Feminism and Philosophy

Perspectives on Difference and Equality

Feminism and Philosophy

Perspectives on Difference and Equality

Moira Gatens

Indiana University Press
Bloomington and Indianapolis

First published 1991 by Polity Press and Indiana University Press

Manufactured in Great Britain

ISBN 0–253–32551–X (cloth)
ISBN 0–253–28190–3 (paper)
Library of Congress card catalog number: 91–72182

Library of Congress Cataloging-in-Publication Data
Cataloging information for this book is available from the
Library of Congress

Contents

Acknowledgements

Many people have contributed to my thinking on various issues concerning feminist and philosophical theory. I would like to acknowledge especially John Burnheim, Elizabeth Grosz, Genevieve Lloyd, Carole Pateman, Barbara Roxon and Marion Tapper, whose writings and/or conversations I have found challenging and inspiring. The Annual Australasian Women in Philosophy Conference has been an invaluable venue, where the contributions of many women have stimulated the development of my thinking over the last decade. I would like to thank the many students who participated in classes I gave on feminism and philosophy at Sydney University, Macquarie University and the Australian National University. Often, I found these classes invaluable learning experiences. The advice offered by two anonymous readers for Polity Press proved invaluable and I am grateful to them for their generous and constructive comments. John Thompson, of Polity Press, also deserves my thanks for his help and patience. Finally, I would like to thank Paul Patton for the many ways in which his assistance made the completion of this project possible.

Introduction

The alliances between feminist and other socio-political theories have often been uneasy. A detailed account of the points of tension in these alliances would require a careful analysis of each particular theory in question. Much feminist research has been of this sort: clarifying the points of tension in the relation between, for example, feminism and psychoanalysis[1] or feminism and Marxism.[2] However, until recently, little work had been done on the tensions *within* the methodologies of feminist theory itself.[3] The question, 'what is feminist theory?' is one that could not be answered without great controversy. There is not *a* feminist theory but feminist *theories*, and if one inspects these closely one finds not so much *feminist* theories as various theories which feminism makes use of or 'borrows', for example, egalitarianism, liberalism, utilitarianism, existentialism, Marxism and psychoanalysis.[4] The feminist theorist may be viewed as a kind of patchwork-quilter, taking bits and pieces from here and there in an attempt to offer an account of women's social and political being that would be adequate to basic feminist principles.

A fundamental premise of feminist theory is that socio-political life – and traditional accounts of socio-political life – are prejudicial to women. Part of the task of the feminist theorist is to offer an account of how the different treatment of the sexes operates in our culture and how the prejudices against women are maintained by economic, social and political arrangements. To this end feminists have attempted to apply Marxism and other theories of oppression or exploitation to the situation of women.[5] This task has been complicated by the fact that these theories were not specifically developed for the situation of women and are often marked by what has been termed a 'sex-blindness'.[6] Feminist theorists re-work these social and political theories in order to remove the sexual biases introduced by male theorists. This approach to the utilization of existing socio-political theories is fraught with difficulties. It assumes that these theories are *essentially* sex-neutral tools that become sexist in their application, in the hands of a Rousseau or a Freud.

The argument of this book is that it is a primary weakness of much feminist theory that it engages with philosophy or theory only at the socio-political level. Such engagement implicitly assumes that metaphysics, theories of human nature and epistemology are sex-neutral.[7] This study will not assume that these areas are sex-neutral. On the contrary, it will be argued that they often provide the theoretical underpinning for the biases which become visible at the socio-political level.[8]

It is necessary, at the outset to clarify the ways in which this study differs from other feminist critiques of the 'sexism' of traditional theory.[9] It is not concerned with the influence of mere (conscious or unconscious) *personal* prejudice. Rather, this study is interested to explore the extent to which there is a cultural prejudice against women that obtains in the very formation of the categories of thought fundamental to modern philosophy. This shifts the accent of the enquiry from the question, 'does this particular theorist hold sexual biases that make their way into his or her system of thought?' to the question, 'do the sexual biases, present in socio-political theories, have their basis in more fundamental categories of thought assumed by political theorists?' If we assume, for the moment, an affirmative response to the latter question, the implications are far-reaching. For, in that case, feminists and non-feminists alike who make use of these theories are, quite independently of their intentions, pre-disposing their studies of society and politics toward conclusions that are prejudicial to women.

Many of the problems of feminist theory are connected to this tendency to be overly trusting of the apparent neutrality of the theory being used. Two texts which have been significant in the development of feminist thought, Simone de Beauvoir's *The Second Sex* and Shulamith Firestone's *The Dialectic of Sex*, both entertain a philosophical dualism of the most orthodox kind that predisposes their work toward locating the source of women's inferior status in female biology. They both accept the mind/body and nature/culture distinctions, treating them as given rather than as social constructions that embody historical and cultural values. To fail to take note of the value-laden character of any particular theory is implicitly to perpetuate the values that have been constructed by a culture that devalues women and those aspects of life with which they have been especially associated, for example, nature and reproduction.

To accept the implicit value system of these theories is to accept the superiority of masculine values and occupations. This is precisely what Firestone and de Beauvoir do in the latter sections of their texts.[10]

Firestone wishes to replace women's reproductive capacity by technical means, claiming that pregnancy is, in any case, 'barbaric'. De Beauvoir also condemns the maternal role. Both theorists posit the necessity to transcend the female body and its reproductive capacities without questioning the ways in which the significance of the female body is socially constructed and its possibilities socially limited.

De Beauvoir sees female biology as a serious limitation on woman's transcendence of 'mere life' into the realm of projects and the creation of values. However, it is necessary to explore the implicit connections within the existentialist framework between attaining an authentic political and ethical existence and the kind of subject assumed able to do so. The politico-ethical stance of the existentialist needs to be examined in relation to the theory of human existence assumed by existentialism and the privilege it accords certain forms of being over others. If transcendence of the body and its immediate needs is accorded a high status then it is likely that women's association with the domestic sphere will disadvantage them in relation to those activities which existentialist politics and ethics take to be valuable.

A counter-argument could claim that de Beauvoir's use of existentialism demonstrates, not women's biological inferiority, but rather the implicit assumption, in the existentialist framework, of a connection between corporeality, immanence and inferiority. Applying this or that theory to women may be viewed as showing the root of women's oppression (for example, her biology), or as showing the limitations of that particular theory when it is applied to women. Existentialism could be understood as showing its limits as an account of *human* life in so far as it can be shown to be only a *partial* analysis of human life with an inbuilt masculine bias. This is to say that the theory can be taken to problematize *women* or women's interrogation of the theory can be taken to problematize the terms of the *theory*.

Thus, a particular theory may be seen, not as a means of explaining or understanding woman's social status, but another factor contributing to this status. In this case, the theory in question itself requires analysis. Much feminist philosophy in the last decade has taken this interrogative stance toward philosophical theories.[11] This stance involves a genuine interchange between feminist theories and past and present philosophies, where each may fruitfully act as interlocutor for the other.[12] Undoubtedly there is much for feminists to learn from epistemology, social theory, and so on, but it is becoming increasingly clear that philosophers who in the past would not have seen feminism as relevant to epistemology or theories of 'human' being are beginning to realize the depth of the prejudices of philosophy and consequently are taking feminist criticisms into account. This introduces the possibility of an ongoing, two-way, productive relation between feminist and other philosophers.

An alternative response to traditional accounts of women's association with reproduction and nature is to acknowledge the inferior value accorded to nature whilst insisting that this value is not an absolute but a social value. Carol McMillan's *Women, Reason and Nature* is a good representative of this approach.[13] She argues that many feminists – and in particular Firestone and de Beauvoir – are no less sexist than the culture they bemoan. She criticizes feminists for accepting the superior value accorded to scientific knowledge and traditional masculine activities and recommends a positive reappraisal of women's traditional roles. Yet McMillan is as uncritical as her antagonists in that she treats the social construction of women as wives and mothers as if these roles were given in nature.

This failure to address the assumptions implicit in socio-political discourses creates a situation where feminists using them are faced with the following choice. Either they affirm a necessary sexual difference resulting in different natures and roles but claim equal *value* for such differences, or they affirm an *essential* equality which will be actualized once women's connection to reproduction is controlled, or severed, by science. In a culture that is dominated by the notion that scientific knowledge provides the paradigm for all knowledge, it is not surprising that these latter theorists would look to science as able to provide 'the answer' to every problem and as promising progress and freedom from 'nature'. McMillan could be identified with the first response to the 'choice' posited above, and de Beauvoir and Firestone with the second.

For all their differences, these three theorists share the assumption of a common problematic within which they take up different positions. This problematic is one which has been constructed around the dichotomies which have dominated modern philosophy: mind/body, reason/passion and nature/culture. Undoubtedly, these dichotomies interact with the male/female dichotomy in extremely complex and prejudicial ways. Attempting to understand philosophical constructions of female and male subjectivities involves, among other things, some understanding of the history of ideas. Confusions and contradictions in philosophy are often the result of historical accretions to terms or conglomerations of terms which cannot be understood independently of their history. These terms can be likened to the mythical chimera whose impossible composition can only be understood if we dismantle its artificial unity and recognize its body as that of a goat, its head as that of a lion, and so on. The association of women with nature, corporeality, passion, emotion and domesticity has a complex history in legal, medical, theological and economic discourses and practices. Philosophy has informed, as well as been informed by, these disciplines. It is not possible to explore these relations here. It is possible, however, to clarify some of the most important connections within the field of modern philosophy between women and nature, women and passion and women and the body. Since it is women who have been so frequently associated with nature and described as prone to the passions which stem from their disorderly bodies, it is crucial to examine the ways in which these associations have been drawn. The historical associations between women, nature, passion and the body are surprisingly influential in contemporary thought. For feminist theory to break and go beyond these associations, an analysis of the way they operate is required.

One of the tasks of this study is to expose the latent commitments in much feminist theorizing to the dualisms of modern philosophy. I am not implying that it is possible to occupy an Archimedean point outside of culture or that it is possible to construct a feminist value-free paradigm, but rather that it is necessary to develop techniques for exposing the latent values in this or that philosophy. The greater awareness one has of what the implicit cultural values of any philosopher's system are, the more power one has to decide what to accept or reject from that system and on what basis such acceptances or rejections rest.

Superficially, conceptions of human nature from the seventeenth century assume a unitary and universal subject. However, an analysis of the paths followed by modern philosophy shows the construction of at least two kinds of human subjects. The apparently sexually neutral human subject turns out to be implicitly a male subject whose 'neutrality' is conceptually dependent on the 'shadow' conception of the female subject. Briefly, we can list some features of these subjects here. The male subject is constructed as self-contained and as an owner of his person and his capacities, one who relates to other men as free competitors with whom he shares certain politico-economic rights. While he has rights to privacy and self-improvement, he relates to women as though they were a natural resource and complement to himself. The female subject is constructed as prone to disorder and passion, as economically and politically dependent on men, and these constructions are justified by reference to women's nature. She 'makes no sense by herself' and her subjectivity assumes a lack which males complete. She is indistinguishable from a wife/mother.

It is the male subject which is most familiar to the student of modern philosophy. It is this self which is most often presented in philosophical works as the *human* being because it is this self which is presented as, in essence, sexually neutral. The agency of this subject is closely connected to its ability to separate itself from and dominate nature. The domination and control of the human body and its needs and desires by the sexually neutral mind sets the terms for modern debates on sexual roles and functions.

From Mary Wollstonecraft through to de Beauvoir and up to the present time, many feminists have connected women's liberation with the ability to become disembodied and transcend 'mere animal functions' and nature.[12] The necessity to be disembodied begs the question of the implicit maleness of the labourer, the citizen, the ethical person. Males can approach the achievement of these ideals only because of the sexed segregation involved in socio-political life. They are able to be 'disembodied' in the public sphere because 'natural' functions, childrearing, sensuality, and so on, have become the special province of women and are confined to the private sphere. The conflicts and compromises involved for women who 'choose' to be both wives/mothers and (paid) workers in the public sphere have no parallel in men's lives.[15] These issues will be treated by way of an examination of various philosophers' writings and the response of feminists (some of whom are also philosophers) to these writings. In presenting a study which looks at men's views on women and women's views on men's views on women, I am aware of the perversity of my position: I am looking at women who are looking at men looking at women. Even when a theorist is herself a woman, the classic structure of taking woman as the object of theoretical scrutiny remains. Women rarely theorize about, examine or look at men. I shall have more to say on this question throughout the book. In the final chapters I attempt to move beyond this classic structure and posit a space that is not dominated by sexual reflections, reversals or inversions. Perhaps that is an impossible space. Nevertheless, the evocation of impossible spaces can unsettle perspectives that have become entrenched, thus making new perspectives possible.

Chapter 1 examines aspects of Rousseau's political philosophy alongside his views on nature, culture and sexual specificity. In this chapter the critique of traditional interactions between feminist theory and philosophical theory will be introduced by examining Wollstonecraft's response to Rousseau. These two themes are continued in chapters 2 and 3 through the discussion of J. S. Mill and Harriet Taylor and of J.-P. Sartre and Simone de Beauvoir, respectively. A primary aim of these chapters is to demonstrate that the feminist critique of the sexual biases apparent in socio-political theories derive their force from fundamental distinctions and assumptions which feminists often leave intact.

Chapters 1 to 3 reveal a variety of ways in which selected theorists have understood the category 'nature' from the eighteenth to the present century. It will be shown that Wollstonecraft, Taylor and even de Beauvoir accept the basic premiss that women are more closely associated with nature. This association encourages the view that the role of wife and mother is women's natural role. This assumption concerning the 'natural' foundation for the sexual division of labour has been challenged only recently by feminist theorists who claim that women's roles are dictated by social and political arrangements and moreover, that the category 'nature' is always constructed from a particular political vantage point. This insight has been significant in determining the directions taken by feminist theory in the last decade and requires close analysis. Why did it take so long for feminists to challenge the so-called natural foundation of women's roles in society? Has this ancient justification been undermined or merely shaken? In the course of the first three chapters the influence of the work of John Locke on the six thinkers considered will emerge. Locke's views will be shown to provide the implicit underpinning to much that is assumed about women's relation to work, property and reason.

Chapter 4 considers the fact/value distinction and its use in feminist theorizations of natural versus social roles. This chapter also considers the thorny issue of the role of language in philosophical discourses by contrasting the work of Janet Radcliffe Richards and Dale Spender. Some appraisal is offered of the writings of Carol McMillan and Mary Daly and their assessments of women's role and status in society. Richards, McMillan, Spender and Daly will also provide contrasting examples of the attempt to *extend* philosophical theories so that they may be appropriate to women (Richards, McMillan) and the attempt to *create* new 'woman-centred' theories (Spender, Daly). Chapter 5 will argue that neither of these options is viable, though both pose problems concerning the methodology of feminist theory. This chapter presents an argument in favour of a dynamic and reflexive relation between feminist theories and philosophical theories, where each acts as interlocuter for the other.

Chapter 6 treats the contribution of psychoanalytic theory to questions of sexual difference, the body and language. In particular, the writings of recent French feminists on the body and sexual difference are considered. Rather than understanding their work as offering a *true* theory of the body, it is argued that their work should be read as offering an understanding of conceptions of the female and male body in *culture* which may be helpful in terms of challenging established associations between women and maternity, women and lack, and of establishing new ones. The aim is to create a terrain where an alternative relation or relations of women to their corporeality may be posited. This aim, in turn, is taken to be co-requisite to the development of a politico-ethical theory and practice that would be appropriate to the contemporary conditions of women's lives.

Chapter 7 considers the way in which the theoretical justifications for women's exclusion from the public sphere, and the consequent collapsing of familial and female interests, are circular or self-fulfilling. Women are constructed as close to nature, subject to passion and disorder, and hence excluded from the self-conscious creation of the body politic which is precisely where nature, passion and disorder are transcended (or, at least, *converted* into *public* goods). The body politic then constructs woman as its 'internal enemy' or, as Hegel phrased it, womankind as 'the everlasting irony in the life of the community.'[16] What a feminist consideration of the history of some of these philosophical conceptions of women and their nature reveals is a basic plasticity or malleability of those conceptions. Conceptions of women are formed, and reformed anew, in accordance with the dominant conception of male subjectivity and its needs. This, of course, has been done from an almost exclusively male perspective, where woman has been conceived only in terms of her relation to man, that is, as wife/mother. This distorted and partial perspective must be challenged by women taking an active role not only in the public sphere of politics and employment but also in the task of theorizing and conceptualizing human life.

1

But for her Sex, a Woman is a Man

1 On 'Becoming Man': the Case of Mlle de L'Enclos

Rousseau was clearly disturbed by the behaviour of men and women in French society and by the influence of modern philosophy which he saw as condoning and encouraging this behaviour. He was particularly distressed by the breakdown of clear sexual differences and often referred to the feminization of men and the masculinization of women with a mixture of disdain and anxiety. Much of his work was directed at the institution of rigid barriers between the sexes in matters of education, social and political life and morals. The corrupting influence of culture he saw to result in a '. . . confusion between the sexes . . .' such that he considered it to be '. . . almost a miracle to belong to one's own sex'.[1] The end result of this trend, he argued, would be to deprive women of their specifically feminine rights, privileges and honours.[2] That he saw the influence of modern philosophy to be largely responsible for this confusion in sexual identities is clear from his remarks concerning a certain Mlle de L'Enclos.

Mlle de L'Enclos was said to have scorn for the specific virtues of women, rather '. . . she practised, so they say, the virtues of a man. She is praised for her frankness and uprightness; she was a trustworthy acquaintance and a faithful friend. To complete the picture of her glory it is said that she became a man.'[3] Rousseau's biting irony is here at its best, and for good reason. His obvious distress at the possibility of women, at least women of a certain class, being considered as equals to men and able to share in hitherto exclusively masculine pursuits fuelled many a sharp diatribe against the social habits and mores of his contemporaries. However, the nature of his writings on women cannot be described as diatribe *in toto*. His work reveals a thorough and, for the most part, consistent line of argument concerning what ought and what ought not to be the function and province of women.

Unlike many of his predecessors,[4] Rousseau does not imply that sex is a mere contingency. Rather, it is one's sex which determines the entire nature and role of the subject, at least if one is female. 'But for her sex, a woman is a man . . .'[5] he writes, yet from her sex follows all else: a different morality; a different education; a different level of access to knowledge and truth; and, of course, an entirely different social and political function from that assigned to men.

Man for Rousseau is both man (on occasions) and the 'universal' subject. His sex does not always or necessarily interfere with his human capacities. Man's possibilities are not tied to time, place or particularity, rather he is able to transcend all these, including his sex, in the apprehension of abstract truths and principles. Woman, by contrast, is always a woman: she is confined by her place, her time, her particularity, her body and passion, in short, her sex. 'The male is only a male now and again, the female is always a female . . .' and, according to Rousseau, '. . . everything reminds her of her sex.'[6] An examination of the means whereby Rousseau lends philosophical justification to the exclusion of women from political life is of particular interest, given that he writes in an era of considerable social upheaval. The body politic of late-eighteenth-century France was undergoing a marked metamorphosis. As recent feminist scholarship has shown, stringent and often brutal methods were used to ensure that women were not admitted to this newly formed political body.[7]

Both Rousseau and Mary Wollstonecraft are commonly associated with the French revolution. Together they provide an interesting contrast concerning what men and women hoped the Enlightenment would achieve. Rousseau and Wollstonecraft will also provide us with an introduction to the historical interactions between philosophical theory and feminist theory. Wollstonecraft's response to Rousseau also provides material for the investigation of the ways in which feminist theory has made use of philosophical theories. What is evident in Wollstonecraft's attempts to challenge Rousseau's stance on women is her tendency to accept his conception of man as the 'universal subject' and to attempt to extend this conception to include women. She offers little by way of critique of Rousseau's philosophical system. Rather, her contention concerns only the place that women occupy within it. This tendency to view philosophical paradigms as sex-neutral will receive detailed comments later.[8] What will be explored in the latter part of this chapter is the attempt by Wollstonecraft, to reintroduce a notion of the sexually neutral subject as against Rousseau's careful specifications of sexual difference. It is significant that Wollstonecraft goes about this task by reiterating certain basic Cartesian principles: that truth is unitary and the same for all;[9] that rationality is what joins women, no less than men, to God.[10] Her argument against Rousseau is that the human subject is, in essence, everywhere and always the same. It is educational and environmental influences which create apparent differences and the effect of these influences, she claims, are nowhere more obvious than in the case of women.[11]

2 'Will the bonds of Convention hold firm without some foundation in nature?'[12]

It is not at all clear from Rousseau's political works, for instance *The Social Contract*, what his views on the place of the sexes in the political and moral spheres are. To discern these views it is necessary to turn to the work he devotes especially to this question: *Emile*. This latter work not only offers valuable insight to the question of sexual differentiation, but is arguably the best summary of his entire philosophy. The answer Rousseau offers to the question which heads this section reveals the foundation for his views on women and men; on passion and reason; and on nature and culture. What I hope to demonstrate by the end of this chapter is that on Rousseau's model of social and political life it is women who are expected to provide the 'natural' foundation necessary for the security and legitimacy of the conventional bond of the social contract. It is the private domestic sphere that provides both materially and emotionally for the continuation of civic society.

Further, Rousseau argues that women should play the additional role of guide or guardian to men; that is, they should, like Ariadne, spin the yarn that guarantees that Theseus will neither come to harm nor lose his way in the maze of culture. Rather, man will retain his relation to nature via his relation to the private sphere, which on Rousseau's account is a kind of 'time-warp' where the 'primitive' and natural patriarchal family is 'frozen'. The retention of this relation to nature is crucial, for Rousseau, in order to avoid the possible development of the corrupting and artificial vices and passions attendant on a highly developed social organization. In other words, provided we do not stray too far from nature we cannot stray too far into error.

One of the most important terminological or conceptual shifts in eighteenth-century philosophy is that from 'God' to 'nature' and from conceiving reason as a hallmark of divine creation to conceiving of reason as a natural development. This shift is most important in the work of Rousseau. What it involves is a change in attitude concerning the influence of culture on the form and development of human subjectivity. Rousseau takes the influence of culture, environment and development very seriously. For him, cultural and environmental differences are not merely unimportant contingencies, rather they are necessary influences on the development of human subjectivity and deserve careful attention.

On Rousseau's account, most of the character of the human being who has left the state of nature is formed by the particular stage or form of social organization in which he or she finds himself or herself. In *Discourse on the Origin of Inequality*, he considers several possible forms of human social development (some historical, others hypothetical) and presents that form which he sees as conducive both to the nature of man (or to his limits) and to the possibilities of his development.[13] The nature of woman and her development is then derived from what is useful to man. As the figure of the tutor in *Emile* says: for man, every question is one of utility, for woman the crucial factor is to conform to social expectation[14] and this social expectation is reducible to what is useful to men. Clearly, for Rousseau, what is most useful to men, and to the continuation of the kind of social organization presented as desirable in *The Social Contract*, is for women to be confined to the primitively (or 'naturally') organized patriarchal family and for men to have access to this private sphere.

The world of the family, infant education, morality and sensuality is private, domestic, whereas the world of work, citizenship, legality and rationality is public. Man's possibilities are predicated on woman remaining static. Susan Moller Okin has remarked on the way in which Rousseau develops the potentialities of man by describing women in functional terms only.[15] The derivation of woman's nature from man's is nowhere more apparent in Rousseau's writings than in *Emile*. This book is most often described as a piece concerned with the philosophy of education. This description does *Emile* an injustice, as it is also a text crucially concerned with political philosophy in its broadest sense.[16] In any case, educating a people or a generation is arguably among the most political of all activities.

At the heart of *Emile* lies the central conflict between nature and culture, between reason and passion, and it is Rousseau's handling of this conflict that determines his views on the proper place of men and women in social and political life. As he writes in Book IV of *Emile*, the difficulties connected with socializing each generation are exacerbated by the fact that '. . . there are so many contradictions between the rights of nature and the laws of society'.[17] It is the reconciliation of these contradictions that Rousseau, or the figure of the tutor, attempts to bring about through the education of Emile. The tutor's task is to be midwife to Emile's birth into culture. As Rousseau observes, 'We are all born, so to speak, twice over; born into existence, and born into life; born a human being and born a man'.[18] This theme of a double birth is also present in *The Social Contract*. It is significant, however, that the birth into culture applies to men only.[19] Women are born only once, born into existence or nature and excluded from culture. According to Rousseau, their natures should be left undisturbed. It is not clear, from *The Social Contract*, that women are excluded in this sense. Rousseau writes there that

> Whoever ventures on the enterprise of setting up a people must be ready, shall we say, to change human nature, to transform each individual, who by himself is entirely complete and solitary, into a part of a much greater whole, from which that same individual will then receive, in a sense, his life and his being.[20]

The apparent neutrality of the language in this quotation disguises what becomes clear only in *Emile*, that is, that entry into civic life is restricted to men only. Women and children are connected to society only indirectly through a father/husband/brother, as is evident from the following extracts from *Emile*: '. . . the family is only connected to society through its head . . .';[21] '. . . when Emile became your husband, he became your head . . .';[22] and finally, 'When you become the head of a family, you will become a citizen of your country.'[23]

This theme of a double birth goes some way toward explaining the disparity between the detailed education of Emile and the rather sketchy comments concerning the education of Sophy. Rousseau is mainly concerned, in *Emile*, with the second birth, that is, the birth into public life and as such he is concerned with men. Women figure in this entry into public life only in so far as '[i]t is not good that man should be alone.'[24] Sophy and her character are important only in so far as Emile's access to the public sphere of citizenship assumes access to a woman; or, more specifically, a wife. It is not that Rousseau is uninterested in the education of women but rather that they should be left as close to their natural state as possible. If necessary, women should be guarded against the ill effects of a corrupt social life and in this task we have the model of Emile's early negative education. The aim of the education of Emile, at least in his youth was 'to prevent anything being done . . .',[25] that is, the '. . . education of the earliest years should be merely negative.'[26] Rousseau extends this maxim throughout the whole of a woman's life. She has no need, on his account, of instruction in the sciences, or in political life. All these aspects of culture are to be managed by men; women's role is merely to reproduce the conditions necessary for the continuation of culture. This involves the bearing, caring and rearing of children and the provision of the emotional and physical well-being of her husband.[27] The most important aspect of these tasks, according to Rousseau, is that they be undertaken in a spirit of chastity, modesty and submission.

In order to determine the possibilities for Emile, it is first necessary for

Rousseau to determine the nature of man. What man can or cannot become is largely determined by what he is in his primitive or original state. In the state of nature, the innate or original passions of *amour-de-soi* (self-love) and *pitié* (compassion) ensure the peaceable coexistence of human beings. Human conflict and strife only arise when these primary passions are perverted by social influence.[28] These modifications of the primary impulse are considered destructive. Man in a state of nature does not need to control his natural impulses, as '. . . the first impulses of nature are always right . . .,'[29] but the moment that he leaves the state of nature and enters society, the dictates of natural appetite can no longer be trusted and Rousseau warns, 'Distrust instinct as soon as you cease to rely altogether upon it.'[30] This view of human nature is what prompts Rousseau to isolate Emile as far as possible from society which can 'hasten the development of the passions'.[31] This isolation, argues Rousseau, will allow Emile's feeling and passion to develop naturally, hence harmlessly, and will further ensure that by the time he begins to be affected by the violent passions (particularly sexual passion) his reason will have developed to a stage that will enable him to control them.

The problem, as Rousseau sees it, is that due to the influence of society man is capable of desires that he does not have the natural strength to satisfy. If nature took its course uncorrupted by social influence, the passions and desires would develop at a rate that man's natural strength would be capable of satisfying. Since we no longer live in this state it is necessary for the educator paradoxically to employ artificial means to ensure natural development. It is only when 'the last and choicest growth',[32] reason, is developed that Emile can be safely admitted into society. Rousseau argues that man's nature is such that, eventually he will be driven from his solitary independence into society with others. It is the precariousness of our existences that draw us together. As Rousseau writes:

> Man's weakness makes him sociable. Our common sufferings draw our hearts to our fellow-creatures; . . . Every affection is a sign of insufficiency; . . . our common needs create a bond of interest [and] our common sufferings create a bond of affection.[33]

It is Rousseau's aim both to allow the development of Emile's natural disposition and yet ensure that he will be a fit member of civil society. This task requires that Emile be made as independent as possible from his fellow men, yet not so independent that he is unable to cohabit with or have respect for them. The tutor engineers several situations to ensure the success of these requirements. The two key aspects of living in a civil society, as Rousseau envisages it, are respect for property and labour, which are intertwined, and the importance of promises. Emile is taught the importance of both these crucial aspects of civil life in the one lesson. This lesson is furnished in *Emile* by some basic instruction in horticulture. Rousseau had already remarked in *The Social Contract* that the actual cultivation of the soil is the only true sign of ownership.[34] In *Emile* Rousseau reinforces this view; as the tutor explains to Emile:

> 'Those belong to you'. To explain what the word 'belong' means, I show him how he has given his time, his labour, and his trouble, his very self to it: that in this ground there is a part of himself which he can claim against all the world, as he could withdraw his arm from the hand of another man who wanted to keep it against his will.[35]

The tutor thus introduces to Emile the pleasure of work and the social mores governing property relations.

Emile is to learn another lesson, however, and one much less pleasant. He is to find out that, unbeknown to himself, though known to his tutor, he has cultivated land to which someone before him has a prior claim. The gardener, who at the same spot was attempting to grow a now spoiled crop himself, informs Emile: '. . . everyone respects other people's work so that his own may be safe . . .'[36] The tutor has thus engineered a vivid lesson for Emile in social rights and obligations. This incident provides the further excuse for Emile to learn the importance of promises and the relation between the worth of a man and the worth of his word. The obvious point of conversion of these rather mundane instances is far from mundane. What the tutor is attempting to instil in Emile is an understanding of the very basis of the social contract. As Rousseau observes, 'Take away the primitive law of contract and the obligation imposed by contract and there is nothing left of human society but vanity and empty show.'[37]

The coping-stone of Emile's development is, of course, his reason, and it is to the proper cultivation of this faculty that the tutor devotes his utmost attention. Reason, Rousseau claims, is not to be cultivated in a pupil by the use of scholarly books, as a book '. . . does not teach us to reason, it teaches us to use the reason of others rather than our own; it teaches us to believe much and know little.'[38] Rather, true reason, 'the reason of intelligence' is based on 'the reason of sense-experience'. In other words, Emile shall not merely be told that two adjacent angles are equal to two right angles, he will be shown that this is the case. In this way, the tutor will once again increase Emile's independence from authority or opinion. Emile will have more than mere knowledge, he will also have a reliable and independent judgement. The power of making reliable judgements is indispensable not only in the arts and sciences but also in matters of morality. When Emile's reason is considered sufficiently developed it is time to introduce him to society and it is in this sphere that his capacity to make accurate moral judgements becomes most pertinent. Sometimes it may be the case that the best judgement is to make no judgement at all or to suspend judgement. This is certainly the case in affairs of the senses or heart, for 'the most dangerous snare, the only snare which reason cannot avoid, is that of the senses.'[39] Rousseau makes it quite plain that he considers the most dangerous sensual snare for men to be '. . . the wiles of wanton women' and from this snare Emile's tutor vows to '. . . guard him with [my] utmost care'.[40]

Emile's tutor is true to his word and takes such care with Emile's dealings with women that he actually chooses a wife for him, unbeknown to Emile.[41] The match is successful and both Emile and Sophy are anxious to marry but Emile has not considered the civil, public consequences of marriage. Sophy does not, apparently, need to. For a man to enter marriage, which is a civil contract, involves duties and responsibilities that Emile had not anticipated. His tutor rebukes him with the following:

> You hope to be a husband and a father: have you seriously considered your duties? When you become the head of a family you will become a citizen of your country. And what is a citizen of the state? What do you know about it? You have studied your duties as a man but what do you know of the duties of a citizen?[42]

Marriage then, for Emile but not for Sophy, involves his proper insertion into the body politic which, in turn, involves certain responsibilities and duties that include, minimally, 'the duty to instruct [himself] in public affairs'.[43]

It is clear from a comment Rousseau makes in *The Social Contract* that he regards marriage as the foundation-stone of civic life.[44] The domestic sphere can support or subvert the public sphere and the responsibility for ensuring that the private sphere supports the public sphere falls on both Emile's and Sophy's shoulders. Their respective duties are different yet equally necessary. By the time Emile returns from his two years of travel, spent familiarizing himself with the governments, laws and people of various countries, he is considered ready for marriage. He is now both a man and a citizen. His education is considered complete.

It may be worth taking stock of Emile's accomplishments and experience in order to contrast these with those of Sophy. Emile, the man-citizen, has a knowledge of man's nature in general, of woman's nature in general and a particular knowledge of his own nature and of Sophy's nature. He can, if necessary, support himself by means of his trade, hence he is independent of the goodwill or charity of men. He has not merely accumulated knowledge but also has an independent faculty of judgement. He is familiar with the morality of his own country and that of other countries, yet he is his own judge in matters of conscience. He is familiar with the arts and sciences, with government, the laws and public affairs in general. In sum, Emile is a man who is independent yet not misanthropic. It will become apparent to what degree Sophy differs from this description.

Sophy's education easily satisfies Rousseau's requirement that 'A woman's education must be planned in relation to a man'.[45] In fact Sophy's nature is formed as the perfect complement to Emile's nature. The strongest single determinant of what her nature should be is given by answers to the question: what would be most useful to Emile both as an individual man and as a citizen? Emile's education, although clearly directed, is designed to allow the development, to the full, of each of his capacities as they arise. The history of Sophy's education is quite different. She will be formed or deformed, overstimulated in some directions, stunted in others, to make her a useful 'help meet' to Emile.

The question of whether Rousseau's account of women is descriptive or prescriptive has been a matter of considerable debate. Okin argues convincingly that the issue for Rousseau is not one of truth but of utility and expedience.[46] He is not concerned with isolated individuals or with abstract metaphysical or ontological questions. Rather, he is concerned with social man and with promoting a certain kind of social organization that is as strong and as long-lived and as equitable (for men) as possible. In this task, Rousseau has several problems to resolve, notably, the tension between reason and passion, culture and nature. One way to resolve this tension is to promote a form of social organization where these aspects of human nature are sexually divided. To Rousseau's mind there is already a basis for this division in nature, that is, women are 'naturally' associated with domesticity and childrearing. Therefore to educate women, regardless of their capacities, to fulfil this domestic role is both 'natural' and reasonable. It is reasonable to do this because of the necessity, in a highly developed society, to separate private concerns from public ones and to diffuse any possible subversive effects of the private on the public. Clearly there are private interests that conflict with the general public interest.

Sophy's education, then, is designed to fit her for the private domestic sphere where the potentially socially disruptive qualities engendered by her education will be privatized and hence converted into qualities that actually support the society by giving patriotism and the love of the laws a basis in nature. This fine line between the construction of women as providing actual support for and possible subversion of the body politic will be discussed later.

It is becoming clearer why Rousseau feared the increasing breakdown of rigid sexual differences. For him the consequences of women entering the public sphere would be disastrous. Either they would 'become men', which would undermine the natural basis of society, or if they remained feminine, they would subvert the body politic. Sophy's education is therefore crucial in that it is she who will provide the basis for civic life. Her teacher is unimportant[47] because she is to be instructed by social expectation. Her reason is to be left uncultivated not because she is incapable of it[48] but because it may destroy those natural feminine qualities that Rousseau sees as so essential to the survival of civil society. As Rousseau pertinently asks: '. . . to make woman our superior in all the qualities proper to her sex, and to make her our equal in all the rest, what is this but to transfer to the woman the superiority which nature has given to her husband?'[49]

To stray too far from this so-called natural hierarchy of the sexes would, on Rousseau's model, mean the end of social life altogether. For, 'if women would discover principles and if men had as good a head for detail, they would be mutually independent, they would live in perpetual strife, and there would be an end to all society.'[50] This is where the artificiality of a highly developed social organization could lead. The basis of Rousseau's fears is here revealed. It is amusing to note the extent to which his doomsday arguments parallel those of his political enemies, the monarchists.

The educational programme set out for Sophy is one which results in the construction of a very precarious subjectivity. Unlike Emile, she is entirely dependent on others for her sense of worth and reputation, in fact for her entire being. It is not sufficient that she be virtuous, she must also be acknowledged as virtuous.[51] Her entire existence is dictated by those around her. As Rousseau observes, ' "What people will think" is the grave of a man's virtue and the throne of a woman's.'[52] By his recommendations for their education, he places women in an impossible situation. They are to be the arbiters of man's pleasure yet exercise restraint over the expression of their own. By making the giving or refusing of sexual favours to men the only power that women have, Rousseau effectively forbids the possibility of women's sexual pleasure. The tutor's parting words to Sophy include the advice: 'You will long rule him [Emile] by love if you make your favours scarce and precious, if you know how to use them aright.'[53]

One of the implications of Rousseau's recommendations is that women do not have access to the passionate and the natural for their own enjoyment but rather they embody the passionate only for the enjoyment of men. It is man who has access to both reason in civic life and passion in the private sphere. Women are excluded from both in that they are neither citizens nor the consumers of privatized pleasure but rather they provide the conditions necessary for men to have access to both.

It is at this point that the significance of the epigraph to this section becomes transparent. Rousseau's argument here is of such importance that it warrants quoting at length.

> I am quite aware that Plato, in *The Republic* assigns the same gymnastics to women and men. Having got rid of the family there is no place for women in his system of government, *so he is forced to turn them into men* . . . but he has not succeeded in meeting the real difficulty . . . I refer to that subversion of all the tenderest of our natural feelings, which he sacrificed to an artificial sentiment *which can only exist by their aid. Will the bonds of convention hold firm without some foundation in nature?* Can devotion to the state exist apart from the love of those near and dear to us? Can patriotism thrive except in the soil of that miniature fatherland, the home? Is it not the good son, the good husband, the good father who makes the good citizen?[54]

Plato's recommendations in *The Republic* concerning the destruction of the family seem entirely unreasonable to Rousseau. On this point Rousseau is perfectly consistent, having observed previously that 'women do wrong to complain of the inequality of man-made laws; the inequality is not of man's making, or at any rate it is not the result of mere prejudice; but of reason.'[55] In other words, the inequalities may well be of man's making but they have their basis in rationality, not prejudice, and moreover, are supported by nature.

To allow the artificial influence of society to alter these 'natural' relations between the sexes would be to stray so far from the natural basis of social life, as to destroy it. It is this destruction that Rousseau sees Plato's recommendations to invite and it is Rousseau's concern for the survival of society that leads him to protest against the behaviour that he perceives to be encouraging the dissolution of sexual difference. Clearly then, on his view, a society that does not enforce rigid sexual difference is a society that will be very short-lived. Having no foundation in nature, such a society would be unstable.

Rousseau allows that no society can survive indefinitely but argues that the longevity of any given body politic, just as with the human body, is directly related to its constitution, in the broadest sense.[56] A healthy social constitution is not to be gained by artificial means but rather by ensuring its basis in nature. Just as Rousseau condemns the artificiality of swaddling babies, which stunts their constitution,[57] so too he sees excessive interference with what he takes to be the natural basis of social life as injurious to the general health of society. This natural basis is the patriarchal family. Rousseau writes, in *The Social Contract*,

> The oldest of all societies, and the only natural one is that of the family; [which can be viewed as] the first model of political societies: the head of the

state bears the image of the father, the people, the image of his children and all, being born free and equal, surrender their freedom only when they see advantage in doing so.[58]

The legitimacy of the social contract is thus assured by an appeal to nature or to a natural order. It is the family that is the basis of social life, which is at the very heart of social life and to suggest the dissolution of the family would, eventually, be to initiate the dissolution of society itself. A mere convention (the social contract) will not survive without its foundation-stone (the natural family).

If the validity of Rousseau's argument is granted, then his proposals concerning the education and social function of men and women gain some plausibility. His political philosophy takes on the form of expediency. It matters not what the 'truth' of woman is, what matters is how to reconcile nature and culture, reason and passion without losing one or the other.

It is Rousseau's partiality for the useful and the expedient that warrants a consideration of his observations on slavery and then to compare this with his views on the social place and function of women. In *The Social Contract*, where Rousseau considers the function of slaves in the Greek state, which he so often admired in his writing, he asks, 'Is freedom to be maintained only with the support of slavery?' and answers

Perhaps. – The two extremes meet. Everything outside nature has its disadvantages, civil society more than all the rest. There are some situations so unfortunate that one can preserve one's freedom only at the expense of the freedom of someone else . . .[59]

This quotation is a particularly interesting one to consider in the light of the several themes that have been raised in this chapter. In Rousseau's account of the transition from the natural and primitive stages of human development to the more advanced stages, the inevitable conflicts between the social and the natural are resolved in three stages. First, by advocating an educational programme that promotes the containment of these contrary aspects of human life by making the natural and the passionate the province of woman and the cultural and the rational the province of man. Second, by an appeal to woman's reproductive capacity, Rousseau presents this division as natural. Finally, by constructing woman as both the natural support for and the possible subverter of cultural life, he justifies her privatization and exclusion from civic life. The submission of woman to this role is further rationalized by the necessity of reason (or man) to govern passion (or woman).

It is the resulting sharp division between the public and the private spheres that lends the appearance of cohesion or 'common sense' to Rousseau's sexual specification of passion and nature on the one hand and reason and culture on the other. The alleged necessity for constant restraint in a woman's life[60] is a direct result of the way in which culture has constructed her. In that Rousseau recommends the construction of woman as, on the one hand, the keeper of socially subversive human passions (she is responsible for both male and female passion) and on the other, as having access to neither privatized passion nor public reason, he constructs her as both dissatisfied and subversive. Hence, restraint becomes necessary to control her dissatisfaction, and her exclusion from the public sphere becomes necessary to forestall her subversiveness. I have attempted to show that Rousseau's proposals concerning the sexes are quite consistent in the terms of his overall philosophical view. This, of course, does not imply that these terms are justified. It is Wollstonecraft, in 1792, who is the first to challenge these terms.

A *Vindication of the Rights of Woman* presents a counterattack to the wide influence of *Emile*, large sections of it being a detailed analysis of various passages from that text. Wollstonecraft's aim may be represented as an attempt to undo theoretically, what Rousseau had done before, that is, she attempts to desexualize reason and passion, nature and culture; to lessen the importance of sexual difference in the structuring of subjectivity and social role; and to *humanize* (or sexually neutralize) both the private and the public spheres. The basis for many of Wollstonecraft's claims is her conception of the sexual neutrality of morality and truth. Her greatest failing can be traced to this source. She does not contextualize human being and human knowledge, and, consequently, she shares many of the problems of Cartesianism, the most striking of which is her conception of a neutral and *a priori* subjectivity. Her unjustified faith in the power of reason and her denigration of the passionate makes her analysis of social life, and the conflicts embedded therein, inadequate.

3 Rousseau and Wollstonecraft: Nature vs. Reason

Wollstonecraft's explicit critique of Rousseau's philosophy is limited to his views on the proper social role and function of men and women, and it is this explicit critique that is most prominent to the casual reader of *A Vindication of the Rights of Woman*. However, a deeper analysis yields a further *implicit* critique of Rousseau's work that stems from the particular view of the role of reason and passion in human subjectivity that Wollstonecraft holds. That this latter, implicit critique is extremely underdeveloped in *A Vindication* is borne out by Wollstonecraft's failure to capitalize on its implications for both Rousseau's stance and her own. This implicit critique will be examined later.

Superficially, *A Vindication* argues for a 'revolution in female man-ners', that is, Wollstonecraft is arguing for a revolution in the way in which the female social role is executed rather than a revolution or change in that role *per se*. She does not, for example, suggest the reorganization or dissolution of the split between the public and private spheres, rather she recommends that both spheres be managed according to the same principles. As she writes in chapter 3,

> Women, I allow, may have different duties to fulfil; but they are *human* duties, and the principles that should regulate the discharge of them, I sturdily maintain, must be the same.[61]

In other words, all human activities should be guided or governed by the same principle: reason. That women do not conduct themselves and their duties rationally may not, she argues, be traced to any innate or natural disposition but rather, to the influence of environment. It is in the area of the education of girls and women that Wollstonecraft seeks to effect changes. Her faith in the capacity of the environment to encourage or dwarf the development of reason stems largely from her utilization of Locke's associational and environmental psychology. Chapter 3 of *A Vindication*, entitled 'The Effect which an Early Association of Ideas has upon the Character', reveals the extent to which Wollstonecraft accepts Locke's *tabula rasa* conception of consciousness. Her argument, follow-ing Locke, is that if you educate girls to be concerned only with their appearance, with trivialities and with the sensuous, then the result is a woman who is vain, trivial and irrational. This form of female education disadvantages not only woman but the entire society as on Wollstonecraft's account the excellence, or otherwise, of a society is reducible to the excellence, or otherwise, of its individual members.

A major disagreement between Rousseau and Wollstonecraft concerns what the purpose or end of education should be. For Rousseau, one of the most important purposes of education is to reconcile the natural with the cultural in such a way that neither is compromised. A successful recon-ciliation of nature and culture ensures, on his account, the stability of the social organization. This conception of education is not one that Wollstonecraft cares to concede. The true purpose of education, accord-ing to Wollstonecraft is to provide '. . . the first step to form a being advancing gradually towards perfection.'[62] To hinder women from this advancement by improper education is thus not only a social injustice; it is also, theologically speaking, to hinder or corrupt the immortal soul.

It is by way of reference to the soul and its divinity that Wollstonecraft attempts to desexualize reason and passion. Contrary to Rousseau, she introduces (or reintroduces) a conception of subjectivity that is in essence sexually neutral. Her conceptions of the soul and passion hold much more in common with those of Descartes than with Rousseau. All souls are alike in their constitution. As a human being is made up of both a body and a soul all human beings, regardless of sex, are susceptible to the passions. In that all human beings have a soul they all have the capacity to restrain the passions by the exercise of their rational capacities. Empirical differences between individuals, and especially between the sexes, regarding the dominance of passion or the dominance of reason are wholly, she argues, an effect of environment and education. Far from instinct being 'always right', Wollstonecraft, preferring the more passive conception, argues that the passions are part of human nature so that we '. . . by struggling with them might attain a degree of knowledge denied to the brutes . . .'[63] Her ontological commitments are quite different from Rousseau's. Wollstonecraft reintroduces the strong distinction between nature and the divine, and clearly, the human subject is located somewhere between the two. What separates a human being from the rest of nature is the capacity for reason.[64]

The explicit critique that Wollstonecraft offers, then, is double-pronged. First, she argues that essentially all human beings start from the same point, all are equally capable of reason, and, second, that the apparent differences between people and between the sexes are the result of environment and education. Her response to *Emile* is to argue that Rousseau is mistaken in claiming a different morality and reason for the two sexes. Rather, Wollstonecraft argues, '. . . the nature of reason must be the same in all, if it be an emanation of divinity, the tie that connects the creature with the Creator.'[65] She further argues that true virtue and morality are possible only from a being who is rational. The argument of *A Vindication* thus amounts to the claim that Rousseau's conception of female morality is incoherent.

According to Wollstonecraft, '. . . the being cannot be termed rational or virtuous, who obeys any authority, but that of reason.'[66] Since virtue is dependent on reason, it becomes crucial, on her account, to educate both sexes according to the same rational principles. The manifest content of Wollstonecraft's reply to Rousseau is to recommend that the principles that he applies to the education of men be extended to the education of women.[67] What she does not take account of is the integral role of Rousseau's philosophy of education to his overall project. Instead, Wollstonecraft argues that Rousseau's recommendations concerning the education of women arise from his own poorly controlled passions.[68] In fact, the educative programme set out in *Emile* is perfectly consistent with the 'egalitarian' principles of *The Social Contract*. As it stands, Wollstonecraft's explicit critique of Rousseau is inadequate to meet certain claims that he makes concerning the necessity to ground the social organization (in particular, the social contract) in nature.

It is the implicit critique of Rousseau's philosophical stance that is likely to be of greater interest to contemporary feminists. This implicit critique can be gleaned by comparing Wollstonecraft's view of human being with that of Rousseau. Clearly, these views are at odds. Wollstonecraft accepts the notion of the perfectibility of human being whereas Rousseau sees conflict and contradiction to be the permanent lot of humankind. According to Rousseau, acting rationally is not sufficient to ensure the resolution of the inevitable contradictions between natural and social human being. Moreover, he sees some human passions and affections as necessary components to the healthy functioning of the body politic. Separate spheres and different 'natures' for men and women are necessary on his view of the relation between nature and culture. It is Wollstonecraft's acceptance of the natural foundation for the sexual division of labour that hinders the development of her implicit critique of egalitarianism. From our perspective, such acceptance is not mandatory. Present theorists are able to question Rousseau's appeal to the 'natural' foundations of social life. Present theorists can address Rousseau's construction of the nature/ culture opposition and the way in which it functions in his pedagogical and political writings. In so far as Wollstonecraft cannot address this problem, her recommendations for extending Rousseau's educative programme for boys to include girls is itself unworkable. Her strategy becomes self-contradictory in that she recommends an educative programme that is designed in relation to a certain view of human nature, held by Rousseau, that directly contradicts her own. Emile's education is predicated directly upon Rousseau's understanding of the conflicts between nature and society, natural rights and necessary social constraints. This understanding of nature and society is not shared by Wollstonecraft.

This tendency to assume the viability of altering what appear to be superstructural parts of a philosopher's work without addressing the foundational assumptions of that work has been common in the history of feminist criticisms of philosophy. The realization of the depth of sexual bias in philosophy has been a long and complex historical process that is far from complete. From our present perspective, the major problem with Wollstonecraft is that she does not go far enough in her criticisms. She presents her views as being in favour of egalitarianism, but against the prescriptions of the egalitarian philosophers, like Rousseau, concerning women. The problem is identified by her as being a problem of individual prejudice rather than being built into the very principles of egalitarianism.

The egalitarian understanding of the relationship between the (natural) private sphere and the (artificial) public sphere assumes a certain view of the division of labour. Specifically, productive labouring relations are moved out of the domestic sphere into the public arena. Domestic tasks are not counted or acknowledged as work, that is, as socially productive and necessary labour. Rather, women's work is seen as part of their natural role, performed in private as a personal service to a particular household. The importance of domestic work to the viability of wage-labouring relations is thus rendered invisible to the public eye. As several feminists have pointed out, the marriage contract holds little in common with wage labour.[69] As the next chapter will show, both egalitarianism and liberalism entertain, from their inception, an explicit connection between citizenship and the ability to engage in publicly defined labouring relations. These relations (between men) are seen to have a *conventional* rather than (as in the relations between men and women) a *natural* basis. This is an important distinction because conventional relations are con-sidered to be mutable whereas natural relations generally are not. This so-called natural division of labour makes women's status as citizens problematical from the start.

It is Wollstonecraft's (understandable) acceptance of the natural foun-dation of the sexual division of labour which makes her conclusion inevitably paradoxical:

> The conclusion which I wish to draw, is obvious; make women rational creatures, and free *citizens*, and they will quickly become good *wives*, and mothers, that is – if men do not neglect the duties of husband and fathers.[70]

This plea leaves unaddressed the marked asymmetry between the citizen/ husband/father and the citizen/wife/mother. Marriage, parenthood and the establishment of a private familial unit do not intrude on men's access to the public sphere. Nor does it deplete their power to act in that sphere; on the contrary, in all likelihood it will enhance their power. The same cannot be said of women. The common response to this asymmetrical access to public labour is to claim that it is women's reproductive capacity that places them at a disadvantage. This response constructs men's and women's place in modern socio-political organization as an *effect* of natural sex differences.

This tendency to conceive of women's bodies as complicit in their social and political oppression has certainly been a feature of much feminist writing. It is a theme that will recur in the work of J. S. Mill and Taylor; de Beauvoir and McMillan. It is a tendency which will be challenged on at least two levels. First, it is necessary to challenge the notion inherited from Cartesian dualism, that human beings are separable into a sex-neutral mind and a sexed body. Second, the imputed naturalness of the form and capacities of the female body must be questioned, along with the idea that these capacities dictate the scope of women's social being. The converse proposition – that social and political arrangements curtail or impede women's socio-political being – must also be considered.

In the next chapter I will consider the way in which sexual specificity is articulated in liberal political theory and feminist responses to this specification. Of particular interest in the following chapter is this tendency to identify the source of women's social status in the female body and to posit the rational and reflective capacities as the means by which this status may be improved.

2

What the Human Species may be Made[1]

Whereas Rousseau argued for the necessity to harmonize human progress and civilization with its natural foundations, John Stuart Mill emphasized the need to transcend that part of human being which is instinctive. For Mill, the human being is a 'bundle of capacities' that requires the guidance of reason for the best of these capacities to be realized and the worst to be extirpated. His disdain for the kind of faith that Rousseau invests in nature is evident from the following comment he makes on the place of the instincts in human progress:

> Allowing everything to be an instinct which anybody has ever asserted to be one, it remains true that nearly every respectable attribute of humanity is the result not of instinct, but of a victory over instinct; and that there is hardly anything valuable in the natural man except capacities – a whole world of possibilities, all of them dependent upon eminently artificial discipline for being realized.[2]

This view of the relation between nature and civilization predisposes Mill toward a dynamic and developmental view of society. Of particular interest here is his sympathy for the emancipation of women. His early and sustained commitment to feminist concerns marks his work off from the traditional absence of women or evident misogyny in the history of philosophy. In some ways this makes Mill's work more, rather than less, problematic. However, it will be argued, if approached in a critical way his work is problematic in a particularly interesting way. A critical appraisal of Mill's attempts to include women adequately in his social, political, economic and moral theory yields theoretical profits far in

excess of the examination of other philosophers who omit these considerations. The profit to be gained from an examination of Mill's work is that
it shows clearly the difficulties involved in applying a supposedly sex-
neutral political theory to women's being.

The theoretical relation between Mill and Harriet Taylor (Mill) will also
be mentioned in terms of the light this relation may throw on past interactions between philosophy and feminism. The debate concerning
Taylor's intellectual capacities and the extent of her contributions to Mill's
theoretical development and productions has been extensively discussed
in the literature[3] and is not of direct relevance here. What is relevant is the
general difficulty that this uncertainty concerning 'ownership' of ideas
presents to the feminist writer.

It is significant that Mill and Taylor were in a personal as well as
intellectual relationship. As was so often the case with 'women of letters',
Taylor's work was easily subsumed by Mill's.[4] One wonders how many
women of astute intelligence have been reduced to the role of 'readers' of
the manuscripts of their husbands. Or, perhaps more pertinently, how
much of women's writing has passed under the authorship of a male name
that was not simply a *nom de plume* but a *nom de mari*. Of course, it is
very difficult to prove whether this kind of 'domestic' service has been
provided since it, like all domestic work, is provided in private. Nevertheless, it is worth noting here that the alleged scarcity of great women
philosophers, artists and writers throughout history can be partly
explained by the invisibility of private services to the public eye. Recently,
feminist researchers have shown how many wives, sisters and daughters
have been private 'assistants' to 'great' male artists, writers and
philosophers.

It is also worth a mention that the way in which female subjectivity has
been articulated in philosophical discourses – for example, the way in
which Rousseau derives Sophy's nature from Emile's – is not unconnected
to the way in which women have related to philosophers. To present an
argument in support of this claim here would be premature. More textual
material is required before such an argument could be presented. In the
last chapter I argued that the basic principles of egalitarianism, as
presented by Rousseau, are such that they prohibit a consistent conceptualization of women as fully fledged citizens of a State that has its basis in
the association of free and equal contractors. I argued there that this
exclusion does not operate merely at the level of application.

Wollstonecraft's attempt to extend Rousseau's political theory to
women, it was argued, substantiates rather than contradicts this claim.
The problem is far more complex than Wollstonecraft's 'solution' admits.
Women's exclusion from the public and civic sphere is an inevitable consequence of Rousseau's theory of human nature rather than a mere political
prejudice. Alternatively, his political prejudice is already embodied in his

theory of human nature. The problem, in any case, concerns the kinds of activities which are considered, both in the history of philosophy and in social practices, as public, and those which are considered as naturally organized private services. This chapter will seek to demonstrate that a similar claim can be made against liberal political theory.

In examining the recommendations of Mill and Taylor concerning what ought to be the place and function of women in socio-political life it will be argued that the failure of liberal principles – as Mill and Taylor present them – to meet the problem of women's subjection is rooted in their universalist view of human nature. The confidence in the neutrality of human being, exhibited by both Mill and Taylor, will be demonstrated to be unfounded. I will be approaching the work of Mill and Taylor by way of three general themes. First, an investigation of their contribution to the debate concerning the precariousness of sexual identity; and second, their implicit assumptions concerning women's bodies. Their assumptions concerning women's bodies relate to those concerning women's work. Given that women are seen to be biologically destined for the role of wife and mother, this role is taken to be natural and so not involving socially necessary and productive work. This second theme is crucial in terms of developing a sustained critique of sex-neutral conceptions of human nature, so prevalent in philosophical discourses. As a corollary to this, the third theme is concerned to demonstrate that Mill, no less than Rousseau, and regardless of his conscious intentions, employs a philosophical paradigm that is intrinsically masculine.

1 The Precariousness of Sexual Identity

> As long as boys and girls run about in the dirt, and trundle hoops together, they are both precisely alike.[5]

Both Mill and Taylor take as negative an attitude to the influence of female culture on men as Rousseau took to the influence of male culture on women. The motivation behind this attitude, however, is quite different to Rousseau's. Far from wanting to promote a form of social organization that would encourage the clear separation of masculine and feminine qualities, the former theorists recommend the means by which women may be brought up to the level of the educated bourgeois male consciousness. Taylor actually argues, and she may well have Rousseau in mind, that:

> Those who are so careful that women should not become men, do not see that men are becoming, what they have decided that women should

be – are falling into the feebleness which they have so long cultivated in their companions. Those who are associated in their lives, tend to become assimilated in character. *In the present closeness of association between the sexes, men cannot retain manliness unless women acquire it.*[6]

Mill is not quite so adamant as Taylor on this point, yet still he advocates the improvement of women lest they have a degenerative effect on men. A central argument for the emancipation and education of women in *The Subjection of Women* has its basis in the necessity for men to progress intellectually, which on Mill's account they cannot do unless women, also, progress. According to Mill it is commonplace that 'young men of the greatest promise generally cease to improve as soon as they marry.' This is accounted for by the effect that the constant association with an inferior engenders. The result is that

he insensibly imbibes the modes of feeling, and of looking at things, which belong to a more vulgar or a more limited mind than his own. This evil differs from many of those which have hitherto been dwelt on, *by being an increasing one*. The association of men with women in daily life is much closer and more complete than it ever was before.[7]

Mill and Taylor then, no less than Rousseau, understand the influence of the sexes on each other to be a serious socio-political problem. This is largely because of the developmental notion of human being that they share. Both have an almost limitless faith in the ability of education and the environment to either hinder or foster progress. The main argument that Mill and Taylor stress in favour of women's emancipation is that the progress of the human race depends on it. To leave women as they are is to halt this progress.

The influence of Locke's conception of consciousness and its contents as reducible to its environment had a significant effect on the way in which the association between the sexes and the influence of this association on behaviour was conceived. This is, in many ways, a novel problem for philosophers: a consideration of the appropriate or rightful place and function of men and women in social, political and economic life. Changes in the domestic, economic and political structuring of families from the eighteenth century highlight this problem.[8] In addition to these changes, and equally significant, is a change in the way human being itself is conceptualized. The way in which human activity and human agency are conceived is reflected in Mill's frequent use of horticultural metaphors in connection with human development and social organization.

The human being is conceived, by Mill and Taylor, as being, initially, a set of organic possibilities whose growth is largely determined by its environment. This is certainly Mill's explanation, as offered in *The Subjection* for the state of women's development. He writes there:

> in the case of women, a hot-house and stove cultivation has always been carried on of some of the capabilities of their nature, for the benefit and pleasure of their masters. Then, because certain products of the general vital force sprout luxuriantly and reach a great development in this heated atmosphere and under this active nurture and watering, while other shoots from the same root, which are left outside in the wintry air, with ice purposely heaped all round them, have a stunted growth, and some are burnt off with fire and disappear; men . . . indolently believe that the tree grows of itself in the way they have made it grow . . .[9]

Mill's criticism of this treatment of women does not pertain to the fact that their 'natural' growth is interfered with but rather pertains to the *nature* of the interference. His short essay on nature makes this point clear. He writes there:

> the duty of man is the same in respect to his own nature as in respect to the nature of all other things – namely, *not to follow but to amend it*.[10]

and

> all human action whatever consists in altering, and all useful action in improving, the spontaneous course of nature.[11]

and, finally,

> the duty of man is to co-operate with the beneficent powers, not by imitating, but by *perpetually striving to amend*, the course of nature.[12]

His argument, then, is that these 'amendments' to nature should not be determined by prejudice, expedience or habit but rather by reason which alone should guide and encourage human development so that it may realize its capacities to the full.

The more influence that reason has in a society, he supposes, the less importance physical strength will have, and, in this state of affairs, women would not be at a disadvantage. Physical strength – which both Mill and Taylor locate as the origin of women's oppression[13] – becomes less important as civilization progresses. This progress involves the development of reason, which is the same in either sex. Hence, the subjection of women, in an advanced culture, has no other basis than habit or custom, both of which are superstitious hindrances to the full development of reason. So the blurring of sexual difference is a necessary corollary, on their account, of human progress. The body becomes increasingly unimportant as the intellect becomes prominent in determining the form and conduct of life. On Mill's account there is no necessary conflict between nature and culture, passion and reason, but rather a progressive climb from one to the other. Nature and passion are the 'seed', to follow Mill's horticultural metaphor, out of which, given the appropriate environmental conditions, reason and culture grow. That women lag behind men in their rational development is a result of the customary and prejudicial manner in which they are raised. It is sufficient, on Mill's account, to alter the environment and the education of women in order to advance them to the stage of development of educated man. Women do not have an inherent or privileged relation to nature or passion. Rather, they have a tenuous relation to culture and reason because of the influence of their surroundings.

This notion of the body as unimportant or irrelevant to the development of consciousness presents a serious problem to the modern theorist who has the benefit of recent psychological research.[14] This research problematizes the basis of the primitive empirical associational psychology that Mill employs.[15] That our experience is *bodily* based is not given sufficient attention in the Lockean conception of consciousness. This omission has further consequences in terms of the use to which this conception of consciousness is put in the socio-political analysis offered by Mill and Taylor. In particular it encourages or allows the plausible presentation of the notion that consciousness is, in principle, sexually neutral. This notion comes about by a conflation of two ideas: first, the insistence on the importance of the environment and education in determining the form and content of human consciousness; and second, the claim that the constant association of the sexes has a levelling influence on consciousness. These two distinct claims become reduced, in Mill's and Taylor's account of domestic relations, to the simple claim that close and constant contact between the sexes will result in a consciousness that is asexual. What is interesting is that they see this potential asexuality of human consciousness as a destructive possibility since the consciousness of women, for historical not inherent reasons, is inferior.

Their project, then, could be described as an effort toward making consciousness sexually neutral, which amounts to minimizing the sexually specific environmental or educational influences on women. Mill and Taylor do not see sexual segregation as the solution but rather propose, in the spirit of Wollstonecraft, the elevation of women lest they debase men.

It is implicit in Mill's conceptualization of human life as progressing from the passionate and natural to the rational and cultural that, if women are to progress then they must become more like men, who typify both the rational and the cultural. This is partly because of the masculine bias inherent in philosophical accounts of reason and culture. This bias is evident in the assumptions made by philosophers concerning which activities count as rational or cultural. The implicit associations between maleness, reason and culture on one hand, and femaleness, passion and nature on the other, must be made explicit and challenged. Until the ground is cleared in this way, superficial proposals for social change only succeed in perpetuating, albeit unintentionally, the very relations they seek to overcome.

In the case of Mill and Taylor, their failure to take adequate account of the cultural construction of women's bodies leads them to duplicate many of the relations that they sought to remove. The problem of women's relation to the domestic sphere is a case in point. Women's domestic functions (childrearing, household management, and so on) are conceived, by both Mill and Taylor, as 'natural' functions. This is inevitable, given their acceptance of the notion that these functions fall outside of culture and can be executed in the absence of knowledge, that is, by 'instinct'. Woman's traditional work is seen to follow automatically from her *being* whereas men's work necessarily involves *doing*, that is, involves rational activity. That both Mill and Taylor understand women's childbearing and rearing capacities in this way is evident from the following comments made by Taylor and Mill, respectively:

> There is no inherent reason or necessity that all women should voluntarily choose to devote their lives to one *animal function and its consequences*.[16]

> It is by devoting one half of the species to that exclusive function, by making it fill the entire life of one sex and interweave itself with almost all the objects of the other, that the *animal instinct* in question is nursed into the disproportionate preponderance which it has hitherto exercised in human life.[17]

An explanation of how this view of women and work reflects a view of human nature that is masculine requires some elaboration and argumentation that belongs, properly, to the next section. For now it is sufficient to note that sexual 'neutrality', at least in the domain of philosophy, frequently involves the reduction of sexual difference to a *masculine* paradigm. This, in turn, involves the allocation of women's traditional work and activity to the domain of nature – a domain that on Mill's and Taylor's view is to be progressively overcome or 'amended' by rational activity. This way of conceptualizing the progress of human culture disadvantages and prearranges the way in which women and their contributions to culture are conceived. It encourages a conception of women as non-rational and as caught in nature by their biology. On Mill's and Taylor's account truly human, as opposed to animal, activities are, by definition, masculine. It is men who embody culture and reason by virtue of the kinds of activities they are involved in: activities that are social, intersubjective and intentional. It is these kinds of activities that Mill and Taylor locate as *human* or rational. The kinds of activities that women, traditionally, have been involved in are, by contrast, seen as natural, as non-intentional and as part of the animal world. This amounts to the claim, which is implicit in the work of Mill and Taylor, that for women to be considered truly human, which involves their progressive dissociation from nature, they must 'become men'.

2 The Body of Woman and Liberal Theory

> every Man has a *Property* in his own *person* . . . The *Labour* of his Body, and the *Work* of his Hands, we may say, are properly his. Whatsoever then he removes out of the State that Nature hath provided, and left it in, he hath mixed his *Labour* with, and joyned to it something that is his own, and thereby makes it his *Property*.[18]

It was argued, in the last chapter, that Rousseau's artificially organized social world depended for its validation and stability on the 'naturally' organized patriarchal family. The social sentiments of patriotism and justice were instilled and nurtured by the various maternal and wifely functions of women. Rousseau thus effectively places women on the side of nature and passion and men on the side of culture and reason and avoids possible conflicts between the two spheres by empowering the public, civic sphere with the ultimate authority. In that Rousseau endeavours to segregate men and women and their social functions, he is not faced with the same kinds of problems that confront Mill and Taylor in their project of sexual integration. Consequently, his political philosophy has a consistency and clarity that Mill's and Taylor's lack. The most glaring problem of Mill's liberal political theory is the difficulty involved in locating women, on an equal footing with men, in the body politic. It will be argued that this difficulty is insurmountable, at least in the terms in which Mill addresses it.

Locke's influence is crucial to an understanding of Mill's articulation of political and civil rights and obligations. Mill's problem, in the crudest terms, is how to make women free labourers. This did not arise in Rousseau's account because of the asymmetrical duties he ascribes to women and men in private and public life. For Rousseau the basis of political life lies in the contracts made between men; women guarantee both the legitimacy and the longevity of public life by the preservation of nature in the private sphere. In that Mill sees no necessity to preserve the nature/culture dichotomy, he sees no need to preserve the distinction between the sexes. On his view, all of culture grows directly out of man's rational transformation of nature. Nevertheless, he confronts the feminist theorist with another kind of problem: the relevance of the philosophical paradigm he employs to the situation of women – in particular to the body of woman and the work of women (these two being historically, if not biologically, tied).

The conceptions of work, labour and ownership evident in political philosophy, at least since Locke, are totally inappropriate as descriptions or accounts of what, traditionally, has been, and often still is, women's work. C. B. Macpherson's summary of the assumptions of the liberal paradigm and its emphasis on individuality and ownership make this point patent. He writes:

> The relation of ownership, having become for more and more men the critically important relation determining their actual freedom and actual prospect of realizing their full potentialities, was read back into the nature of the individual. *The individual, it was thought, is free inasmuch as he is proprietor of his person and capacities.* The human essence is freedom from dependence on the wills of others, and freedom is a function of possession. Society becomes a lot of free and equal individuals related to each other as proprietors of their own capacities and of what they have acquired by their exercise. *Society consists of relations of exchange between proprietors.* Political society becomes a calculated device for the protection of this property and for the maintenance of an orderly relation of exchange.[19]

What is evident from Macpherson's succinct summary of the basic tenets of liberal theory is that they function against an assumed backdrop of market relations. In neither a legal[20] nor an economic sense could women be seen as sole proprietors of their persons or capacities in a market relation. Men are socio-economically placed such that Macpherson's description is a theoretically coherent account of relations between men as individual owners of their persons and free contractors of their capacities. Women, however, are not analogously placed and in the sense described above cannot legitimately be described as individuals at all. As Macpherson stresses, the individual is constituted as such by virtue of his ownership of his body and its capacities. His freedom is predicated upon this proprietorship. The relations of exchange that govern a capitalist economy are, implicitly, relations between *men* that have as their support and guarantee a domestic and familial organization that defies description in 'free' market relation terms.

The mode in which domestic work is conducted is qualitatively different to the mode of public production: for example, by virtue of the absence of a wage relation. This fact raises the necessity for a *different* kind of analysis of women's social and political existence. Mill does not take account of this. This is largely because, in following Locke's conception of what constitutes *human* labour and his conception of the relation between labour, property and rationality, he fails to recognize domestic work as a *social* or *cultural* activity. Rather, he sees it as a 'natural' or lower-level activity that makes possible social labour between men, and under certain conditions,[21] between women. This misconception of domestic work as naturally rather than socially organized is further augmented by the popular misconception that it is work that is historically invariable. It does not involve the exercise of what Mill would call the 'higher faculties' such as reason, but is rather a statically unvarying exercise of the instincts.[22] The way in which Mill understands women's subjection is largely in terms of their relegation to these 'animal functions and their consequences'. He does not see that it is the *social* organization of these functions, and the social attitude reflected in Mill's own description of them, that both constitute and help to perpetuate the undervaluing of women and their *cultural* contributions.

Mill understands progress to be linked to the control and emendation of nature, that is, to the transcendence of nature through rational activity. For this reason he sees the changing relation of men to their environment (as evidenced say, in the transition from feudalism to capitalism) as progressive in character. It is progressive both in terms of the greater mastery over nature and in terms of the dramatic alterations these changing relations to the natural world effect at the level of political and economic organization. As he writes in *Utilitarianism*:

> The entire history of social improvement has been a series of transitions, by which one custom or institution after another, from being a supposed primary necessity of social existence, has passed into the rank of a universally stigmatised injustice and tyranny. So it has been with the distinctions of slaves and freemen, nobles and serfs, patricians and plebeians; and so it will be, and in part already is, with the aristocracies of colour, race and sex.[23]

This quotation is interesting for what it overlooks. These historical relations between men – of slave and freeman, noble and serf, patricians and plebeians – each involved distinctive differences between the sexes. Male and female patricians, for example, did not have the same rights or political status. Male and female slaves were used by their masters in quite different ways. Even if one envisioned a socio-political system which treated men and women *identically*, it is highly unlikely that the result would be desirable or equitable. Some acknowledgement of the differences involved in male and female embodiment seems crucial if the political body is genuinely to 'represent' both men and women. This issue will be given detailed treatment in chapter 7. For now, it may be noted that Mill's excessive rationalism is most visible in relation to the question of the necessarily asymmetrical roles of men and women in the reproduction of life, and importantly, the *cultural* dimensions of women's work.

Regardless of whether women wage-labour or not, it is they who are traditionally responsible for the early socialization of children. Unless this activity is acknowledged as work, that is, as transformative rational activity, the subjectivity of woman will be automatically classified as more animal and less human than man's subjectivity. Women's place in cultural life has only recently been acknowledged as requiring theorization. This acknowledgement has generally been of the kind that gestures to the *absence* of women in dominant theorizations of social, political and economic life. This difficulty can be traced to the masculine nature of philosophy itself, that is, that it has historically reflected, almost exclusively, male experience and interest. The relatively recent access of women to philosophy involves the gradual exposure and eroding of this bias.

A central argument of this study is that women's contribution to philosophy cannot be merely an 'adding on' of theorizations of women's experience but rather involves a radical reconstruction of basic assumptions in philosophy. The definition of work as the rational or intentional transformation of the natural environment by men is one such assumption that requires redefinition. We need to furnish a conception of work that will be coherent as an account of the diversity of *human*, rather than just masculine, activity. As long as women's traditional activities are not seen as work, that is as socially necessary labour and as labour that is *social*, the justification for the patriarchal structure of the family and its role in sustaining the structure of the public sphere will remain unquestioned. It is quite explicit in *Emile*, for example, that male access to a woman's body and labour is crucial to his functioning as an efficient citizen. Emile does not become a citizen proper until he has some understanding of political life which is centred around and sustained by the patriarchal family unit. It is assumed, in liberal political theory, that the citizen is an *individual* who is also a husband/(potential)father; that is, who has at his disposal the services of a domestic worker in order that he be free to compete efficiently on the labour market. This aspect of liberal theory becomes most apparent when Mill writes of women and wage labour. It is on the question of women and work that Mill and Taylor diverge most radically and for this reason will be treated separately.

Mill intends to bring women up to a par with men *in principle* only. In other words, Mill argues that women should be given the same educational and vocational training as men but, under 'normal' circumstances, these capacities would not be actualized by (married) women since they have the already demanding tasks of childrearing and household management. Mill's insistence on women's economic independence is almost entirely one of principle. This is revealed by his comment that 'it does not follow that a woman should *actually* support herself because she should be *capable* of doing so: in the natural course of events she will *not*.'[24] His justification for this is two-fold. First, he thinks that it is undesirable to increase the labour market[25] and, second, he raises the difficulties for women of a 'double-shift'.[26]

To what then, does this educational and economic equality, in principle, amount? It is clear from Mill's comments concerning a mother's task of childrearing and a wife's contribution to the standard of family life that he does not consider either to require ratiocination. Women's primary occupations involve *being* rather than doing, as is evidenced by the following passages:

> The great occupation of woman should be to *beautify* life: to cultivate, for her own sake and that of those who surround her, all her faculties of mind, soul and body; all her powers of enjoyment, and powers of giving enjoyment; and to diffuse beauty, elegance and grace everywhere . . .[27]

This, on Mill's account, is her 'natural task', . . . 'if task it can be called, which will in so great a measure be accomplished rather by *being* than by *doing*'.[28] Similarly, the socializing role of women in childrearing is considered by Mill to involve the 'imperceptible and unconscious' infusion of their person throughout the environment of the child rather than an active tutelage. The education proper of the child should, where possible, be left to trained educators. Mothers should be concerned with the *moral* training of the child. In Mill's words:

> The education which it *does* belong to mothers to give . . . is the training of the affections: and through the affections, of the conscience, and the whole moral being. But *this* most precious, and most indispensable part of education does not take up *time; it is not a business, an occupation.*[29]

Undoubtedly, it would be difficult to calculate the time involved in childrearing on a labour market model. This does not, however, imply that it involves *no* time but rather that it is not a task analogous to other forms of employment or occupations that are governed by a market economy. In much the same way the work, activity or effort involved in ensuring an emotionally and psychically comfortable environment, for both husband and children, cannot be measured in terms of capitalist calculations of labour time.

It is this 'invisibility' of the social and political functions of the domestic sphere in a capitalist economy (and the consequences of this invisibility for women) that renders Mill's suggestions for the achievement of sexual equality vacuous. His argument, that if married women were *capable* of being economically independent then this would change their situation from that of 'an odalisque, or of a domestic servant' to that of a free and rational individual, is *practically* untenable. At best what Mill's recommendations concerning the improvement of the relation between the sexes would result in is that married women would be dependent not only financially, but also intellectually on their husbands. He does not, in either the early essay on marriage or in the mature *Subjection*, consider the possibility of women's full integration into public life, unless in exceptional circumstances.[30] His mature view remains disjunctive: either women marry, in which case their functions are domestic, or they remain single and live their lives in the public sphere in a manner not unlike men. As he writes in *The Subjection*:

> Like a man when he chooses a profession, so, when a woman marries, it may in general be understood that *she makes a choice* of the management of a household, and the bringing up of a family, as the *first* call upon her exertions, during as many years of her life as may be required for the purpose; and that *she renounces*, not all other objects and occupations, *but all which are not consistent with the requirements of this*.[31]

Mill's liberty 'in principle' for women is based on an unconvincing notion of consent and choice. As the above quotation reveals, the 'choice' of motherhood, once made, takes precedence over any other 'choices' or commitments in one's life. He also assumes that most women would make the choice of motherhood and domesticity over wage labour. It is Mill's conception of childrearing responsibility as falling 'naturally' to women that puts the issue of 'choice' or 'consent' on precarious ground. This view of domestic work, coupled with a close reading of part 4 of *The Subjection*, encourages the suspicion that Mill is not so concerned with the emancipation of women *per se* but with the *benefits* to mankind that would be brought about by a change in the *manner* in which women conduct their traditional tasks, a change consistent with liberal capitalist society. He again and again stresses the importance of the moral influence of women on both husbands and children. The negative moral and intellectual influence that he understood the vast majority of women (the 'hostages to Mrs Grundy') to have on their families has been mentioned above. It is in part 4 of *The Subjection* that Mill is most scathing in his attack on the conservative and degenerative influence of women and one is reminded of his attacks, in *On Liberty*, on the tyranny of public opinion which tends to promote the mediocrity he deplored. Concerning this influence he writes:

> The wife's influence tends, as far as it goes, to prevent the husband from falling below the common standard of approbation of the country. It tends quite as strongly to hinder him from rising above it. *The wife is the auxiliary of the common public opinion.*[32]

If this section of *The Subjection* is read in tandem with Mill's ethical views as espoused in *On Liberty*, I believe we come closer to his motivation for advocating what amounts to little more than a version of Wollstonecraft's 'revolution in female manners'. He writes there that the most important consideration in ethical matters is utility, '. . . but it must be utility in the largest sense, *grounded on the permanent interests of man as a progressive being.*'[33] It is clear that at the present stage of human development, Mill regarded capitalist society as the form of social organization most conducive to these 'permanent interests'. Mill's opposition to socialism (which at least offers the *possibility* of the socialization of domestic work) is largely in terms of what he saw as its inhibitory effects on individual incentive and competition, both of which he regarded as crucial to the development of the individual.[34] However, in that this individuality is predicated on the ownership of one's person and capacities, it effectively excludes married women to whom the market-oriented notions of 'competition' and 'incentive' are inappropriate.

This primary concern with the individual as a developmental being, which runs through all of Mill's writings, acts as a sovereign term in that it subjects all other issues that come under his consideration.[35] It is clear that this preoccupation is the major obstacle to recognizing that the domestic organization of women's lives, and the relation of the domestic sphere to the public sphere, is the crux of the problem of women's emancipation. The fact that Mill intends leaving both structurally intact involves little more for women than liberty *in principle* and an obligation to acquire *and retain* a form of rationality that, even considered in Mill's own terms, would be exceedingly difficult, given the character and concerns of the domestic environment.

In fact, what women are meant to provide in Mill's liberal utilitarianism is much the same as that which he conceived Harriet Taylor to provide in his own life. His disillusionment with Bentham's version of utilitarianism concerning its lack of emphasis on feeling and emotion is reflected in Mill's attitude towards women and what he saw as their positive talents. His suggestion of the 'equal' but 'different' complementary roles of the sexes in marriage and in culture presents problems because, clearly, these differences are not arbitrary. Women excel in the moral, the practical and intuitive skills; men in logical and abstract skills and in the formulation of principles. Whether or not his is an accurate general description of men and women in Western culture is not the point. Rather, the point is to examine how these 'qualities' are engendered, perpetuated and pre-arranged with differential values.[36]

In a manner that alarmingly parallels Rousseau's derivative account of women's nature and utility, Mill intends to use women's 'skills' to balance what he saw as the sterility of cold, analytic, abstract reason; the preponderance of which, in his own life, he located as the source of his mental crisis.[37] The full utilization of the 'grace', 'beauty' and naturally inclined 'practical bent' of women were, on Mill's view, crucial to the progression of civilization.[38] Mill, no less than Rousseau, has a derivative notion of 'what woman ought to be' that reflects the employment of a paradigm that is, in principle, a *masculine* one. This claim will be elaborated in the next section. For now, a consideration of Taylor's views on women and work and how these views differ from Mill's is in order.

Unfortunately, a fair consideration of Taylor's views is hampered by the fact that there are only two short articles by her that are flawed by underdeveloped or incomplete argumentation. It is possible to suppose that one can recognize (intuitively) in Mill's writings ideas or comments that seem more characteristic of Taylor's thinking than of Mill's. We also have Mill's assurance that most of what he wrote after 1840 was a 'joint production'.[39] However, neither intuition nor Mill's insistence constitute a definitive demonstration of Taylor's contributions to works published under Mill's name alone. For now I will be content to point out the ways in which Taylor's views on the emancipation of women conflict with and are more radical than Mill's. Yet, her views exhibit a 'blindness', analogous to Mill's, to the political and social significance of domestic work.

Taylor's views, on both marriage and women's rightful place in the public sphere, display an extreme distaste for the extent of legislative power in the life of the individual. This distaste surpasses even that of Mill. According to Taylor, all laws relating to marriage and the strictures operating in relation to the occupation of any public office or profession, should be abolished.[40] She argues

There is no need to make provision by law that a woman shall not carry on the active details of a household, or the education of children, and at the same time practise a profession, or be elected to parliament. *Where incompatibility is real, it will take care of itself* . . .[41]

This argument is all well and good, in principle, but the liberal failing so evident in Mill is also in evidence here. Implicitly, what they both argue is that wealthy women may combine a profession with marriage because they are able to employ *other women* to perform the domestic functions attendant upon marriage and childrearing. This amendment to social and political life may well result in the partial emancipation of a certain class of women but cannot be considered as a serious proposition for all, or even most, women.

The same bias towards the bourgeoisie is present in Taylor's proposal in relation to children. Once all laws relating to marriage were abolished, the responsibility for children would fall wholly on women, such that '. . . if a woman had children she must take charge of them, women *could not* then have children without considering how to maintain them.'[42] Again, this effectively involves, at least under a capitalist economy, the restriction of the option of childbearing to an elite few who have either 'independent incomes' or the means to enable the employment of a surrogate mother.

What is interesting about Taylor's proposal here is that it poses a theoretical if not a practical threat to patriarchal property relations and through this to the particular political and economic character of the society she addresses. The suggestiveness of some of her proposals may encourage one to take seriously Mill's claims, in his introduction to the posthumously republished 'Enfranchisement of Women'. He states that the issue of women's emancipation '. . . in her [Taylor's] opinion, was in a *stage* in which no treatment but the most calmly argumentative could be useful, while many of the *strongest arguments were necessarily omitted, as being unsuited for popular effect.'[43] This interpretation of the restrained radicalness of Taylor's proposals gains further support if one considers the extent to which she shared Mill's views on both the progressive nature of civilization and the ability of certain exceptional individuals to see beyond the stage of civilization that they inhabit. Clearly both Mill and Taylor considered themselves as two such individuals.[44]

There are passages in the 'Enfranchisement of Women' that support the claim that Taylor viewed capitalism as an impermanent phase[45] and that her proposals for the achievement of sexual equality were limited by and tailored to the exigencies of a capitalist economy. As she argues,

> so long as competition is the general law of human life, it is tyranny to shut out one-half of the competitors. All who have attained the age of self-government have an equal claim to be permitted to sell whatever kind of useful labour they are capable of for the price which it will bring.[46]

Neither Mill nor Taylor, however, ever raises the question of domestic work as a form of 'useful labour'[47] or the possibility of the socialization of such work, though it is very likely that they were both familiar with this idea.[48] The location of women's subjection in the resilience of what they both conceive as a 'customary prejudice', overlooks the political aspects of the privatization of women and domestic work. This is a question that neither theorist addressed.

Mill's solution is unsatisfactory in that it poses an exclusive choice for (bourgeois) women of marriage/motherhood or public labour, except in those rare cases of genius and wealth which may allow the maintenance of both roles. Of course, women of the working class did not have the luxury of such a 'choice'. Taylor's solution of combining both roles, though more radical in the sense that it presents a threat to the public/private division, results practically in doubling women's workload. Clearly both writers are limited by the socio-political structures with which they are compelled to work. It may well be that to suggest the socialization of domestic duties is simply utopian and, moreover, fails to address the concrete social, political and economic situation. This is not, however, the main thrust of my argument. Rather, my criticism concerns the way in which they both view the private sphere as women's natural realm; the domain of 'animal functions and their consequences', on the one hand, and the public sphere as the realm where men engage in rational, cultural and transformative activity, on the other.

This link between rationality, masculinity and proprietorial relations needs to be addressed much more directly than either Mill or Taylor could have done. Certainly Taylor comes close to an implicit acknowledgement of the equation, in a capitalist economy, between access to the political realm and participation in public production when she argues, against Mill, for the necessity of women to enter the labour market. Even if this entailed that '. . . a man and a woman could not together earn more than is now earned by the man alone.'[49] This would be preferable to the situation of most married women which, she argues, can only be described as domestic slavery. This partial acknowledgement of the connections between social value, power and public labour is, however, still far from satisfactory. It leaves unquestioned the connections between private domestic labour and public labour and the dependence of the latter on the former.

So while Mill's proposals tend to conservatism in terms of their *structural* effects on the situation of women, Taylor's proposals tend to effectively impose another structure (that of wage labour) over the domestic one, thus doubling women's work and responsibilities. Both proposals are unsatisfactory for the same reason. Neither challenges the differential conception of women's work as instinctive, natural and animal and men's work as cultural, human and rational. What requires explanation here is how, in liberal theory, the rational comes to be tied with property and public production.[50] An explanation of this phenomenon is crucial in this context because, for both Mill and Taylor, the cultivation of rationality and individuality is synonymous with freedom and human progress. In the following section I argue that these very terms – rationality, individuality, freedom, progress – which are foundational to liberal theory, are not neutral, human categories but rather presume a subjectivity that is inherently masculine.

3 Liberal Theory as a Masculine Paradigm

> The only part of the conduct of anyone for which he is amenable to society is that which concerns others. In the part which merely concerns himself, his independence is, of right, absolute. *Over himself, over his own body and mind, the individual is sovereign.*[51]

The right of the individual to the pursuit of liberty and progress is acted out, in liberal theory, against an assumed background of certain kinds of labouring and ownership relations. These relations are, implicitly and historically, relations between men.[52] In this section it will be argued that these relations between men are made possible by, and sustained by, the political and economic subjection of women. In other words, the free-enterprise 'equality' between men necessarily excludes the participation of women *on an equal footing*. Finally, it will be argued that, because of the inbuilt masculine prejudice of liberal theory, the attempt by Mill and Taylor to extend this equality to women unwittingly produces an ideal of human excellence that women cannot possibly actualize.

Mill's conception of history and human progress is characterized by a steadily increasing alteration and control of nature that frees the individual from the base necessities of life, which may be met by the exercise of the 'lower faculties' alone, and allows the cultivation of his 'higher faculties'. It is only by the cultivation and exercise of these 'higher faculties' that true human happiness, perfection and, eventually, truth can be attained.[53] The principles of liberal philosophy are appropriate to a certain stage of human development and their utility is to be found in their tendency to bring the progress of human beings '. . . nearer to the best thing they can be'.[54] It is clear from Mill's understanding of so-called primitive societies that he does not view liberal society as a form of social organization that can be applied to any society ahistorically. He describes 'primitive' societies as '. . . those backward states of society in which the race itself may be considered as in its nonage . . . Liberty, as a principle, has no application to any state of things anterior to the time when mankind have become capable of being improved by free and equal discussion.'[55]

It is only in more advanced societies, where rationality rules, that liberalism can function appropriately. The progress of civilization entails the prominence of reason and mental strength over passion, the instincts and bodily strength. For a society to reach the age of 'free and equal discussion' involves the development of man's relation to nature to such a stage that he is able to exercise his higher, rational faculties to attain ends that would have, at a prior stage, involved the exertion of lower capacities such as brute strength. In this transition power comes to be attached to rationality, that is, initially, to the ability to labour effectively, efficiently and, hence, to accumulate wealth.

This implicit assumption of a connection between rationality and ownership is important to the present concern in the following way. Mill argues, in both *Essay on Marriage and Divorce* and in *The Subjection*, that the origin of women's subjection is their physical inferiority. In an age when physical strength equalled power, women were disadvantaged. His claim is that, given physical strength is no longer related to political power in this way, then there is no basis for women's continued subjection other than 'artificial feeling and prejudice'.[56] Two things, Mill argues, mark the progress of civilization. The first concerns the unimportance of physical strength to social power. He writes

> Every step in the progress of civilization has tended to diminish the deference paid to bodily strength . . . *The strong man has little or no power to employ his strength as a means of acquiring any other advantage over the weaker in body.*[57]

As, for Mill, the subjection of women has its origin in the relative weakness of their bodies, this growing unimportance of physical strength leads to the second characteristic of progress, which is '. . . a nearer approach to equality in the condition of the sexes'.[58] One of the problems with this explanation is that Mill overlooks the fact that women are still disadvantaged, even though they are no longer excluded by the criterion of physical strength, in that power now becomes associated with wealth and property. Given that, in a patriarchal society, women are restrained by the demands of the private sphere and often disadvantaged by the rules of patriarchal inheritance, they actually have *less* power than previously.

As social value and power come to be increasingly associated with ownership and *public* production, women's work and subjectivity comes to be characterized as 'primitive', as concerned only with 'animal functions'. As such, it is work that is unpaid. It is the amendment of nature through rational labour, and the resulting independence from other men brought by proprietorship and wealth, that constitutes individuality for Mill.[59] The problem is still centred, then, on women's traditional work and its relation to social and economic value. Women's historical development, economically and politically, is not analogous to men's historical development. The problem both Mill and Taylor confront is how to bring women's economic and social status in line with men's. This is why Mill stresses the necessity for women to acquire the *power* of earning and Taylor stresses the *necessity* of earning. However, in that neither of them directly question the bases of capitalist property relations, and the supportive role that women and their labour in the domestic sphere play in these relations, they end by positing little more than an ideal that women can never actualize. It is an ideal that is based on the 'freedom and equality' of men in market relations that in turn presupposes the unpaid labour of women. To attempt to bring women 'up to' the stage of labour market relations to ensure their equality with men without questioning the domestic basis of these relations is tantamount to either doubling women's workload (Taylor's proposal) or obscuring the political and economic functions of the domestic sphere (Mill's suggestion).

There is a third 'option', which is for women to 'become men', that is, for women to function in the public sphere 'as if' they are men. However, even this option disadvantages women, both individually and as a group. It disadvantages women individually in that they do not have the benefit, as do their competitors, of an unpaid domestic worker. It disadvantages women as a group in that if they do not reproduce they are not able to consolidate and accumulate wealth through inheritance. So the irony of Mill's and Taylor's concern with 'the individual' is that they fail to see that 'the individual', because of the very assumptions built into the notion of individuality, is *male*. In their attempt to emancipate women they produce a model of human excellence that is, inherently, masculine. These covert assumptions which encourage the equation of the human *par excellence* with masculinity will be of increasing concern for the remainder of this study. It is quite obvious in de Beauvoir's writings that for women to become truly human they must aspire to masculine qualities. Much feminist writing has, albeit unconsciously, accepted this equation at face value. In the following chapter I will be considering what this has involved for the interaction between feminist theory and existentialism.

What the principles of liberalism, as presented by Mill and Taylor, amount to when applied to women is that until women 'assimilate' masculinity they are a brake on progress, because progress involves the actualization of masculine qualities. Just as Wollstonecraft failed to locate her objections to Rousseau's philosophy at the level of the supposed universalism of egalitarianism, so too do Mill and Taylor fail to note the inappropriateness of applying liberalism to women. They fail to consider questions concerning the manner in which particular body politics construct women: their bodies; their relation to nature; and the products of their labour. Women's labour certainly transforms what it works on, but in no sense could such transformation or embodiment of women's labour be said to create relations of ownership.

Children and husbands – as objects/subjects of women's labour, for example – cannot be said to be 'owned'. This problematizes women's relation to their power to labour. Do they 'own' even that power? Once again, the point of the argument and analysis offered here is to demonstrate that liberalism, no less than egalitarianism, cannot be regarded as a sex-neutral paradigm. The apparently neutral conception of the human body and its relations to the environment that they employ is a conception based on European, bourgeois male experience and activity. It is an inadequate conception of the female body and its historically and culturally determined relations to work, to the environment and to other human beings. The effect of this inadequacy is to place women, in spite of Mill's and Taylor's intentions, back into the 'natural' sphere of domesticity. In this sphere work appears as 'natural' – that is, as not-work – and as following 'naturally' from women's being.

It is now clear why the issue of sexual difference/inequality most often makes its appearance in the field of political theory. What I have attempted to show is that attempts by feminists or feminist sympathizers, such as Mill, to tackle these inequalities only at a political or economic level are unfruitful because of an unnoticed circularity. For example, when Rousseau asks 'What is man/woman?' he is not asking a question in a political void. He has in mind the preservation of a particular set of political and social relations that determine how he answers this question. This is why there is such a strange discrepancy in the work of Hobbes,[60] Locke[61] and Rousseau[62] between their descriptions of men and women in a state of nature, on the one hand, and in the body politic, on the other. All three assume an equality between the sexes in the pre-social or pre-political state. Sexual difference does not become significant to these theorists until reproductive and other relations between the sexes become matters of concern to a polity. It is when reproduction and women's nature are considered in this political context that philosophers tend to treat women's roles in terms that are functional and teleological. This hidden political agenda, which underlies philosophers' discussions of women's nature, is present in Mill's writings too when he asserts, in *Essay on Marriage and Divorce*, that 'The question is not what marriage ought to be, but a far wider question, *what woman ought to be*'.[63] The language that Mill uses here reveals the purposive and teleological nature of his question. He asks not 'what is woman?' or 'what could she become?' but rather 'what *ought* she be?'. It is not an open question but rather a politico-ethical one, and his answer to it assumes a female nature that is already politically structured.

3

Woman as the Other

In chapters 1 and 2 arguments for and against women's right to liberty and equality have been presented. Simone de Beauvoir's *The Second Sex* positions itself as a study anterior to these questions of rights and liberty. In the introduction she writes that her study is animated 'less by a wish to demand rights than by an effort towards clarity and understanding.'[1] Rather, she seeks to address the harmless looking question: what is woman? In particular de Beauvoir seeks an answer to the question: why is woman the perpetual Other? Part of what makes it possible for de Beauvoir to ask this open question concerning woman is the philosophical perspective which she employs: existentialism. As is well known, the particular form of existentialism employed by de Beauvoir is that developed by Jean-Paul Sartre in *Being and Nothingness*.[2] Here I will simply mention some salient features of that philosophy which bear on de Beauvoir's use of it.

Unlike the philosophers we have considered thus far Sartre rejects any notion of an *a priori* or essential human nature underlying, conditioning or limiting the possible forms of social and political life. His famous maxim, 'existence precedes essence'[3], involves a commitment to the radical nature of human freedom. The meaning, values and character of human life are all to be explained in terms of free human creation. This theory would then seem to be appropriate to a genuine consideration of women's social and political possibilities. If there are no fixed natures then there is no 'eternal feminine' which dictates women's social role as wife/ mother. Moreover Sartre explicitly states that his phenomenological existentialism is an attempt to overcome the dualisms of mind and body, nature and culture, central to traditional philosophical accounts of human ontology.[4] This feature of existentialism would also encourage one to think that it is a theory which would not automatically condemn women to the realms of the body and nature. Presumably, these aspects of existentialism are what compel de Beauvoir to put aside her 'hesitation' and take up the 'irritating' subject of woman.[5] At last, after centuries of spilled ink on the subject, it is possible to approach it with clarity and sense and it is existentialism which makes this possible.

However existentialism also harbours its biases against women. The values that existentialism espouses turn out to be no less antagonistic to women's possibilities than other theories we have considered. Its presuppositions, it will be argued, are such that women, their traditional activities, their bodies and their subjectivities are rendered problematical relative to men, their pursuits, and their bodies.[6] De Beauvoir wastes no time in telling us what these philosophical presuppositions are:

. . . our perspective is that of existentialist ethics. Every subject plays his part as such specifically through exploits or projects that serve as a mode of transcendence; he achieves liberty only through a continual reaching out towards other liberties. There is no justification for present existence other than its expansion into an indefinitely open future. Every time transcendence falls back onto immanence, stagnation, there is a degradation of existence into the 'en-soi' – the brutish life of subjection to given conditions – and of liberty into constraint and contingence. This downfall represents a moral fault if the subject consents to it; if it is inflicted upon him, it spells frustration and oppression. In both cases it is an absolute evil. Every individual concerned to justify his existence feels that his existence involves an undefined need to transcend himself, to engage in freely chosen projects.[7]

We see de Beauvoir here employing the familiar terms of existentialist philosophy, central to which is the opposition between transcendence and immanence, an opposition that highlights the difference between human being and mere animal or species being.

The existentialist perspective maintains that human being is a mode of being between being and nothingness. Put another way, human being distinguishes itself by its constant reaching beyond its present state into an indefinitely open future. What we become, what we make of ourselves, is conditioned not by history, biology or an innate human nature but rather by our own free acts. Sartre maintains that we are not free not to be free, we are 'condemned' to this endless making and re-making of ourselves. These free acts, to which we are condemned, constitute our transcendence, our projects or exploits in the world. Unlike non-human animals we are not mere 'en-soi' (being-in-itself), we are not reducible to our brute existence. Rather human being, in that it lacks a determined nature, is able to transcend 'mere being' in its creation of human meaning and values. What de Beauvoir names 'a moral fault' in the above passage, Sartre refers to as 'bad faith'.[8] He argues that the free human consciousness, faced with the awesome responsibility of forever creating itself anew, will inevitably experience anguish or nausea. One possible avenue of escape from this anguish is to utilize the ambiguity of my being. Human being is both a transcendence (a being-for-itself) and an immanent facticity (the 'en-soi', or being-in-itself). By affirming myself as an immanent facticity (for example, I just *am* a thief, or a coward), I avoid having to face my future possibilities, that is, I deny my transcendence. This is to put one-self in bad faith and is what de Beauvoir is referring to above as a moral fault.

In the context of the concerns of *The Second Sex*, a woman who claims that marriage, motherhood and dependence on a man are her *only* possibilities, rather than a freely made choice, would be in bad faith. The Sartre who wrote *Being and Nothingness* allows of no other possibilities: human subjects are either *authentic*, that is, they accept the nothingness at the centre of their existence and live with the anguish of that state; or they deny their freedom, their transcendence, by putting themselves in *bad faith*, that is, by acting as if something other than their own free choice determines their being. It is important to note here that de Beauvoir inserts a third term into the bad faith/authentic opposition: the term 'oppression'. Thus, it may indeed be the case, for some women, that marriage, motherhood and dependence are all that their material conditions allow. In terms of de Beauvoir's analysis then, these individuals are neither authentic nor in bad faith, rather they are oppressed.

Many critics of Sartre's early formulation of existentialism argue that Sartre does not pay enough attention to social and political forces in his account of human freedom. His theory of existence is a particularly individualistic one which does not take sufficient account of social *structures* and the effect of these structures on the formation and develop-ment of human consciousness. Sartre later addressed this problem himself in *Saint Genet: Actor or Martyr* (1964) and, especially, in *The Critique of Dialectical Reason* (1976). Nevertheless, at the time of the writing of *The Second Sex*, existentialism had little or nothing to offer by way of a social theory. It is to de Beauvoir's credit that she manages to intro-duce the structural or social element into existentialist theory without thereby having to abandon it altogether. Yet, as will be shown, the intro-duction of the notion of oppression gives rise to several confusions and inconsistencies in her account of woman's being. These problems, in turn, cast some doubt on the explanatory power of existentialism in the field of social analysis – problems that eventually came to trouble Sartre himself. A sub-theme of this chapter then, is to show the kind of dialectic at work in the interaction between feminist perspectives and philo-sophical perspectives. Existentialism allows de Beauvoir to examine, in a novel light, the situation of women, whilst, at the same time, such an examination demonstrates the inadequacies of existentialism as a theory of *human* or social, rather than *male* or individual, being. I do not here mean to suggest that de Beauvoir explicitly sets out to demonstrate the inadequacies of existentialism. Quite the contrary, it is by taking seriously its own claims to be a universally applicable theory of human being, that she, albeit inadvertently, exposes its masculine bias and limitations.[9]

Returning to de Beauvoir's main concerns in *The Second Sex*, she asks, from the perspective of existentialist philosophy, 'what is woman?' and 'why is she defined as the Other?' Clearly, from the perspective she employs, 'woman' cannot be defined by a changeless essence. In so far as woman is a human being, she, no less than man, is an ambiguous 'becoming'. Consistent with the existentialist commitment to the essential openness of human being, de Beauvoir rejects any account of woman which seeks to reduce her to her biological function ('*Tota mulier in utero*') or to any reductive psychological theories based in these functions. Predictably enough, de Beauvoir takes these aspects of woman's situation as telling us only about her facticity, not her freedom. Her second concern, 'why is woman the perpetual Other?' is the more complex one. Following Hegel and Sartre,[10] de Beauvoir maintains that 'Otherness is a fundamental category of human thought' and

> we find in consciousness itself a fundamental hostility towards every other consciousness; the subject can be posed only in being opposed – he sets himself up as the essential, as opposed to the other, the inessential, the object.[11]

This fundamental hostility of consciousness is not the problem; nor is the hostility between the sexes a problem in itself since it is to be expected that 'the duality of the sexes, like any duality, gives rise to conflict'.[12] Rather, the problem is to find out why, transhistorically and cross-culturally, woman consistently occupies the position of Other. It is only to be expected that woman should be man's other and man, woman's other: this is already implied by the duality between the sexes. This dual relation, however, should be a *reciprocal* one: maintained 'sometimes in enmity, sometimes in amity, always in a state of tension.'[13] What requires explanation is woman's fixed status as the absolute Other and man's occupation of the position of absolute Subject: why is there no reciprocity in the relation between the sexes?

On de Beauvoir's account there is no single explanation of this phenomenon. The character of woman must be understood in the context of her entire situation. Many factors conspire in the final outcome. Yet even this is a misleading way to talk since 'woman today' is never a completed reality, never a finality. De Beauvoir is careful to insist on this point:

> When I use the words *woman* or *feminine* I obviously refer to no archetype, no changeless essence whatever; the reader must understand the phrase 'in the present state of education and custom' after most of my statements. It is not our concern here to proclaim eternal verities, but rather to describe the common basis that underlies every individual feminine existence.[14]

Woman's situation, like that of any existent, is ambiguous, open to change. In fact:

> An existent *is* nothing other than what he does; the possible does not extend beyond the real, essence does not precede existence; in pure subjectivity, the human being *is not anything.*[15]

The future, then, is open to women, it is the 'not-yet' which will unfold only through their own acts, decisions and choices. But human being is not simply a 'pure subjectivity'. Both man and woman, in addition to being individual subjects, are also participants in a 'species being'. De Beauvoir follows both Freud and Marx here in stressing this double function of human life. It is in this context that woman emerges from her study as *biologically* disadvantaged. The female body is: 'prey to the species'; 'locked up in its immanence'; 'in the iron grasp of the species'; to a much greater degree than the male. The views presented in *The Second Sex* on the female body are quite subtle and easily misinterpreted. It is not the case that for de Beauvoir biology can *determine* woman's situation since she must take up an attitude to her own embodiment. This attitude, which is not determined by biology, will decide whether the female body is lived in shame and discomfort or whether it will be affirmed as the ground of free action.

Biology cannot, in the context of existentialism, have any *a priori* significance: it is always that which is to be interpreted; that which is to be lived by the free consciousness. The situation is further complicated, however, in that biology is lived in a historical and social context whose meanings must also be deciphered. Hence, an understanding of woman's situation requires a study not simply of biology, but also psychology, history and sociology. These areas are treated by de Beauvoir in Book I of *The Second Sex*. Book II examines these aspects of woman's situation through a phenomenological and literary examination of the variety of ways in which women may experience themselves – the adolescent, the mother, the lesbian, the wife, the independent woman, each share in the feminine predicament, yet each 'lives' it differently. This is to say, simply, that each woman makes the feminine condition her *own* condition through living its significance in a more or less unique and subjective way.

The meaning and capabilities of the female body are particularly important in the context of existentialism since it takes the body as the phenomenological ground for all human action. On de Beauvoir's view, it would seem that this ground, in the case of the female body, presents a problem. Woman's reproductive role binds her to species life to a much greater extent than the male. There is the constant suggestion that such involvement in the reproduction of life *a fortiori* excludes women from participation in culture and from the production of values. Perhaps even more crucially, such suggestions throw doubt on the very possibility of affirming the female body as the ground of free action. Some examples of this view follow:

> Here we have the key to the whole mystery. On the biological level a species is maintained only by creating itself anew; but this creation results only in repeating the same Life in more individuals. But man assumes the repetition of Life while transcending Life through Existence; by this transcendence he creates values that deprive pure repetition of all value . . . [woman's] misfortune is to have been biologically destined for the repetition of Life . . .[16]

> Woman, like man *is* her body; but her body is something other than herself.[17]

> It is quite true that woman – like man – is a being rooted in nature; she is more enslaved to the species than is the male, her animality is more manifest . . .[18]

> Her body does not seem to her to be a clear expression of herself; within it she feels herself a stranger.[19]

> Not to have confidence in one's body is to lose confidence in oneself. One needs only to see the pride young men take in their muscles to understand that every subject regards his body as his objective expression . . .
> *Her* whole body is a source of embarrassment.[20]

Now, it is clear from other passages in *The Second Sex* that de Beauvoir is fully aware of the way in which neutral biological 'facts' can be turned into loaded social *values*. Taboos concerning virginity, menstruation and childbirth, for example, make sense only against a backdrop of male privilege. These significances often weigh heavily on a young girl seeking to find her place and value in the social world to which she has been born. All this is not to say that the female body is an *intrinsic* liability.

However, in the above passages, de Beauvoir is committing herself to much more than an acknowledgement of the effects that oppressive social meanings can have on the way one lives one's biology. She is also making some highly contentious remarks concerning the effects, on women, of their greater involvement in the reproduction of the species. Her argument presupposes that the individual consciousness is opposed to his or her species being. In the case of men this opposition is minimal: he is most likely to feel it in the process of ageing where his biological being may become a hindrance to his projects and aims. For women, however, the opposition between her species being and her individuality is posed as constant and debilitating. Such involvement in the reproduction of 'mere life' prevents women from conceiving and executing projects; rather she is trapped in a body – which she often does not fully accept as her own – that is condemned to repeating life rather than providing a ground from which to create value. Hence, she lives her body as a burden, as a stranger, as something other than herself.

It is certainly true that de Beauvoir stresses that biology can have no hold on an individual transcendence. The form and capacities of the female body can not *alone* hold woman back from the formation of transcendent projects. She comments, in this context, that 'if the biological condition of woman does constitute a handicap, it is because of her general situation.'[21] Yet this does not alter the fact that for de Beauvoir female biology, considered in isolation, is in conflict with the individual subject. Sexual desire, reproduction and familial life do not constitute handicaps for men. It is women's involvement, at the biological level, with these aspects of human life that conspire against the fulfilment of her projects *as an individual*. Moreover, this 'handicap' is not wholly socially produced; it has its basis in the materiality of the female body. It is, then, this materiality of the female body – in addition to the social disadvantages of being a woman – which must be transcended.

On de Beauvoir's view such transcendence involves taking the female body as an object of knowledge for science: it is gynaecological knowledge, after all, that has allowed women to escape from the 'iron grasp' of the species. At this point we may begin to wonder what difference employing the existentialist perspective has made to developing alternative ways of thinking about the possibilities of women. De Beauvoir, in a fashion reminiscent of the writings of J. S. Mill and Taylor, concludes that in order to achieve authenticity, woman must overcome or transcend her biology and her role in natural life. By this means, she enters the culture which has excluded her as a creator of values. Man's material existence presents no such problem. Even in the pursuit of 'biological' aims he transcends their nature as mere repetition by making them *his* aims. Man's species being and his individuality can both be satisfied without undue conflict or sacrifice.

It is clear from de Beauvoir's descriptions of primitive and nomadic

societies that she sees man's relation to nature as involving, almost necessarily, transcendent action. Women were confined to the domestic tasks
'because they were reconcilable with the cares of maternity'. These tasks,
in turn, 'imprisoned her in repetition and immanence'. Men, in contrast,
'furnished support for the group', not through mere 'biological behaviour,
but by means of acts that transcended his animal nature . . . To maintain,
he created, he burst out of the present, he opened the future' and created
value.[22] This account begs the question of what de Beauvoir means by
cultural values and the overwhelming masculine nature of these values, as
she describes them. Consider the following comments:

> For it is not in giving life but in risking life that man is raised above the
> animal: that is why superiority has been accorded in humanity not to the sex
> that brings forth but to that which kills.[23]
>
> . . . giving birth and suckling are not *activities*, they are natural functions;
> no project is involved; and that is why woman found in them no reason for a
> lofty affirmation of her existence.[24]

These comments do not sit very comfortably with others that she makes
which stress that human being is lived always in a context of socially
produced meanings and values. Clearly, in a patriarchal society, activities
which women only can perform are unlikely to be highly valued – but
this is not her claim in the above passages. Her claim is that motherhood is
a 'natural function' that is tied to animal existence and hence immanence;
the very 'symbol of immanence', for her, being 'the female belly'.[25] On this
understanding, reproduction and childrearing cannot constitute *projects*
for women. De Beauvoir assumes that in order for woman to take up a
project, that is, to assume the position of a transcendent subject, she must
first transcend the female body. We will return to this question of the
transcendence of the female body – which, as we will see, is the task of
culture as well as of women – when we consider her views on history. At
this point it is sufficient to note that de Beauvoir analyses the female body
in terms not simply of its otherness to man, but also in terms of its otherness to woman herself.

    The otherness of the female body, for both sexes, takes on a special
significance at the level of psychology and feminine sexuality. It is this
body and its capacities, after all, that 'justifies' the restraint and passivity
that society expects from feminine behaviour. The young girl will feel her
activity frustrated not only by external social forces, she will also experience the 'shame' and discomfort of menstruation; bear most, if not all, of
the responsibility surrounding pre-marital courting rituals; and finally, in
marriage, will find that transcendence is now possible for her only vicari-
ously, through her husband and children.

It is in the life of the young woman that de Beauvoir sees the conflict between species being and individual being to be most strongly in conflict. Again, this conflict does not find its correlate in the male sex:

> The young man's journey into existence is made relatively easy by the fact that there is no contradiction between his vocation as human being and as male . . . But for the young woman . . . there is a contradiction between her status as *a real human being* and her vocation as *a female* . . .[26]

What does this statement involve, if not agreement with male privilege when it asserts that to be 'really human' is to be a male? De Beauvoir's views on male and female sexuality do little but reinforce this masculine view of sexual difference.

> The sex organ of a man is simple and neat as a finger . . . but the feminine organ is mysterious even to the woman herself, concealed, mucous, and humid as it is; it bleeds each month, is often sullied with body fluids, it has a secret perilous life of its own . . . Feminine sex desire is the soft throbbing of a mollusc . . . man dives on his prey like the eagle and the hawk; woman lies in wait like the carnivorous plant, the bog, in which insects and children are swallowed up.[27]

It is difficult to read this description of the female body without recalling Sartre's descriptions, in *Being and Nothingness*, of the 'sliminess' of the in-itself and the threat it poses to the for-itself.[28] He writes there that 'Slime is the revenge of the in-itself. A sickly-sweet, feminine revenge . . . a soft, yielding action, a moist and feminine sucking . . .'.[29] Femininity is here associated with that which threatens to engulf transcendence and degrade it to the level of mere 'sticky' existence. De Beauvoir shares this view of femininity as 'the Other' that threatens the free consciousness with its cloying and 'appealing' nature. According to Sartre the feminine sex is 'obscene' because it 'gapes open' and 'is an appeal to being as all holes are'.[30] The danger in answering this appeal, however, is that one may be 'swallowed up'.

Sartre's influence on de Beauvoir's conception of the female body and femininity is quite clear. What is equally clear, however, is that she does not hold that woman, in any essential sense, is doomed to this femininity or to the dictates of female biology. Man has taken advantage of woman's greater involvement in mere species being, making of her the absolute Other, and woman, giving in to the temptations that confront every existent, has often been complicit in this. However, human being is not static. It is lived differently in different historical periods, under very different political, economic and social conditions. It may well be a historical fact that women have been disadvantaged in the past. However history has no hold on human reality since:

> historical fact cannot be considered as establishing an eternal truth; it can only indicate a situation that is historical in nature precisely because it is undergoing change.[31]

Knowledge of, and control of, the female body have made it possible to insert a wedge between female biology and woman; between femininity and woman.

'Women today' are no longer bound to the species as were our fore-mothers. It is in the present context *only*, that one can say of (presumably, Western) women who affirm their *necessary* connection to the female body and femininity, that they 'commit a moral fault' or that they are in 'bad faith'. It may well be these women de Beauvoir has in mind when she writes, in the Introduction, that some women do not assume the status of subject because they are 'often well pleased with [their] role as the Other.'[32] These women's actions cannot, on de Beauvoir's analysis, be seen as simply individual cases of moral failing. They also represent a brake on human progress and particularly on the progress of the relation between the sexes. Here again we find echoes of J. S. Mill and Taylor. The inferiority of women may well have had some basis in the past but in the present time any such inferiority has the status of superstition. Historical associations between women and femininity have little force in our current context. Hence, de Beauvoir's announcement, on page 107 of *The Second Sex*, that 'The devaluation of *woman* represents a necessary stage in the history of humanity'[33], can become, by page 728, 'the devaluation of *femininity* has been a necessary step in human evolution.'[34] By this stage of her text, the work of undoing any *necessary* connection between 'woman' and 'femininity' has been completed.

It is now open to women to participate in culture, to work and create 'on the same terms as men'; indeed, modern women accept 'masculine values'[35] and are enjoined to 'unequivocally affirm their brotherhood'[36] with modern man. It is important to note, however, that women's participation in this fraternity is predicated on her repudiation of the female body and femininity. A symmetrical repudiation of the male body and masculinity is not in evidence in the case of men's participation. On the contrary, the male body and masculinity are covertly taken to be the norm. Something of this sort was seen to be operating in our consideration of the liberal subject in the last chapter. We will return to this issue again in chapter 7.

At this point we certainly need to pause and take stock of what de Beauvoir has achieved by her employment of the existentialist perspective.

It is undeniable that she was one of the first, if not the first, to make a viable distinction between woman's biological sex and the way that sex is lived in culture – a distinction which would now be signified by the sex/gender distinction. This work is invaluable in terms of separating women's *social* or *historical* existence from her *possibilities*. The existentialist perspective, it seems to me, was a crucial factor in the successful completion of this task. However, this distinction can be made without assuming the masculine perspective along with its denigration of the female body and femininity.

The moves made by de Beauvoir in her disentanglement of the three terms 'femininity', 'the female body', and 'woman' echo Sartre's views on knowledge and nature and female embodiment. Sartre, like Freud, sexualizes human knowledge: knowledge is fundamentally structured by curiosity concerning 'the other sex'. But, again like Freud, this knowledge and this curiosity amounts to the curiosity of the male concerning the female. Sartre names this structure of knowledge the 'Actaeon Complex', after Actaeon who gazed upon the naked Diana. In Sartre's words:

> If we examine the comparisons ordinarily used to express the relation between the knower and the known, we see that many of them are represented as being a kind of *violation by sight*. The unknown object is given as immaculate, as virgin, comparable to a *whiteness*. It has not yet 'delivered up' its secret; man has not yet 'snatched' its secret away from it. All these images insist that the object is ignorant of the investigations and the instruments aimed at it; it is unconscious of being known; it goes about its business without noticing the glance which spies on it, like a woman whom a passerby catches unaware at her bath . . . Every investigation implies the idea of a nudity which one brings out into the open by clearing away the obstacles which cover it, just as Actaeon clears away the branches so that he can have a better view of Diana at her bath.[37]

The object of de Beauvoir's investigation *is* woman so perhaps we should not be too surprised that 'woman revealed' is the outcome. Yet, her investigation also purports to show why woman is the absolute Other of culture and here, we find de Beauvoir sharing the male perspective, perhaps not on the question of woman, but certainly on the question of the female body and femininity.

What emerges from her investigations is that the female body and femininity quite simply *are* absolutely Other to the human subject, irrespective of the sex of that subject. Her critique of the masculine viewpoint is that man does wrong to collapse 'the female body and femininity' together with 'woman'. In the past this conflation may have been justified but, in the present context, it is no longer justified. There is no *necessary* relation between female biology and what women are capable of doing or becoming. There is no *necessary* relation between femininity and woman. Therefore, woman today can escape the appellation of the absolute Other provided that she also escapes the female body and femininity and takes them as her (absolute) Other. The female body is other to her humanity, her subjectivity, in short, to her transcendence, which can be asserted only on condition that she escapes the grip of the female body. Man and woman may, at the level of consciousness, each be the other's other but the absolute Other remains essentially feminine.

This is why *The Second Sex* directs Diana's gaze toward her own body, not Actaeon's. The fraternity, which de Beauvoir hopes to see established between men and women, will be 'a reciprocal relation of amity' that will put an end to the quarrel between the sexes. This reciprocity is itself, however, based on the transcendence of femininity, for 'the quarrel will go on as long as men and women fail to recognize each other as equals; that is to say, *as long as femininity is perpetuated as such.'*[38] The perpetuation of masculinity, given its associations with transcendence and progress, emerges from de Beauvoir's study as a value in itself.

The Second Sex displays a problematical asymmetry between its treatments of the cluster: femininity, the female body and woman, on the one hand, and masculinity, the male body and man, on the other. This asymmetry raises the question of whether the existentialist framework is capable of adequately addressing the task which it has been set. In this way – leaving aside the benefits mentioned above of the employment of the existentialist perspective – de Beauvoir demonstrates the points of tension and intellectual dishonesty at work in that perspective. If existentialism purports to be a theory of human being, yet its values emerge as sexually biased, then it must forfeit its status as a universal theory. Moreover, if its values are able to be asserted only at the expense of the other, it will be an intellectually dishonest perspective. Ironically, in Sartre's own terms, such a perspective could only be held in bad faith. This is, after all, precisely the stance of the anti-Semite, who is Sartre's paradigm example of the figure of bad faith.[39]

4

Language, Facts and Values

In the last chapter it was argued that de Beauvoir's use of existentialism in her appraisal of women's situation presents several difficulties for contemporary feminist theorists. In particular, it was argued that the implicit associations between transcendence and the formation of rational projects, on the one hand, and immanence, the body and nature, on the other, perpetuate a bias against women. Historically, it is women who have been associated most closely with nature and the body. This criticism reveals the extent to which the very language of existentialism involves an implicit bias against women. It is not a sex-neutral philosophy.

Formulating an adequate response to the biases in philosophical theories is one of the most difficult issues in contemporary feminist theory. On the one hand we have those who suppose that these biases are superficial. Others suppose that philosophical theories are irremediably patriarchal and insist that what is required are new theories which take women's experiences as their foundation. These are the two most obvious strategies to employ in the face of the biases of philosophy: remove the bias or condemn and reject the theory. In this chapter I will consider four responses to this issue: Janet Radcliffe Richards's *The Sceptical Feminist*, Carol McMillan's *Women, Reason and Nature*, Dale Spender's *Man Made Language* and Mary Daly's *Gyn/Ecology: The Metaethics of Radical Feminism*. My reading of these responses seeks to demonstrate both the inadequacy of treating philosophical theories as unproblematic standpoints from which to criticize feminism (Richards and McMillan) *and* the inadequacy of treating women's experiences and perspectives as capable of providing a 'pure' standpoint from which to create new 'woman-centred' theories (Spender and Daly). Chapter 5 will argue in favour of another option.

It may be appropriate to add a note here concerning a criticism commonly directed against contemporary feminist philosophy. It is often claimed that much academic or philosophical feminism is elitist, 'too theoretical' and inaccessible to the vast majority of women. This and the following chapter will indirectly respond to this criticism. First, by showing that simplistic or 'obvious' responses to philosophical traditions are inadequate. Second, by sketching tried and failed responses to sexual biases in philosophy, I hope to show why it is that much contemporary feminist philosophy is concerned to explore language and signification, epistemology and methodology, and psychoanalysis and deconstruction. Hopefully, when contemporary feminist theory is placed in a historical context, with its various turns and detours signposted, it will lose much of its alleged obscurity.

Two issues stand out in the contrast between the work of Richards and McMillan, on the one hand, and that of Spender and Daly, on the other. First, the question of whether language is sex-neutral; and second, the widely held distinction between matters of fact and matters of value. Both McMillan and Richards agree that feminists fail to treat the fact/value distinction adequately. For both theorists it is important to 'get the facts straight' before tackling the issue of value; and feminists are accused of confusing these two levels. Both are sceptical about the credentials of the feminist project. They present themselves as Athena-like figures who aim to civilize the feminist Furies and bring them to reason. McMillan and Richards repeatedly cast feminists in a rather 'unattractive' light, chastising them for their shoddy reasoning (and even, in the case of Richards, for their shoddy appearance!).

Another, more disturbing similarity between Richards and McMillan is their tendency to treat feminism as a monolithic position. They frequently use expressions such as 'feminists believe', 'feminists argue', 'feminists claim', and so on. Little acknowledgement is given to the great variety of political, epistemological and ontological commitments amongst feminist writers. They seem unaware that liberal, Marxist and radical feminists may have differing and often incompatible responses to such fundamental questions as: 'what is human nature?'[1] This similarity may be partially explained by the fact that both writers display a scant acquaintance with feminist theory, as their bibliographies attest. McMillan seems to take Firestone as the spokeswoman of the movement, while Richards's sources are often obscure. Much of the latter half of her text is constructed as a response to hearsay concerning what some feminist or other purportedly said or did.[2]

It will be argued that both McMillan and Richards frequently conflate two levels of feminist analysis: the level on which feminist theorists have argued against existing social arrangements; and the level on which feminist theorists address the deeper forms of conceptualization which underlie social and political attitudes toward women. It is one thing to criticize current political practices for excluding women from equal representation and participation in decision-making procedures. It is another to point out that, throughout its history, the bourgeois state explicitly denied such participation to women and as a result has developed in a lop-sided way. Since women's interests have historically been limited by their confinement to the private sphere, it is difficult to see how present concerns of women can be articulated within a public sphere which has been defined against the private sphere. These are problems that cannot be overcome by ensuring equal, formal access to the public sphere. They require the difficult and complex analysis of the public/private dichotomy itself.[3] Both Richards and McMillan seem unable to distinguish these two distinct levels of analysis.

1 Firm Foundations

Richards modestly claims to do for feminism what Descartes did for philosophy: set it upon 'firmer foundations'.[4] Her definitions of both feminism and philosophy are extremely narrow. Feminism is defined as the belief that 'women suffer from systematic social injustice because of their sex' and anyone who accepts this definition is counted as a feminist.[5] On her view, feminism is primarily concerned to eliminate 'a type of injustice'.[6] This definition puts a good deal of strain on the terms 'justice' and 'injustice' and it is not until chapter 4 that Richards clarifies these terms. I shall say more about her conception of justice below. One important effect of defining feminism in this way is that it serves to neutralize the radical theoretical challenge that feminists have presented to traditional notions of politics, and to such terms as justice.

Much of the work of feminists has been concerned to illustrate the ways in which the history of the development of terms such as 'rationality', 'power', 'freedom' and 'justice' involve the exclusion of traits associated with women. The argument here is that it is not simply that women do not empirically measure up to the ideals of humanity held by philosophers, but that these ideals are themselves inconsistent with cultural ideals of femininity or womanhood.[7] Richards's text is unwilling or unable to engage with feminist critiques at this level. She prefers to focus on one aspect of contemporary feminist concern (inequitable legislation) that is amenable to treatment by way of liberal political principles. As a result, Richards's conceptual analysis is limited to working within existing systems of conceptualization, while her political responses are limited to those changes that could be brought about within the parameters of existing liberal society. The very terms in which she defines and constrains feminist theory make her treatment of it both shallow and distorted.

Richards chooses to assess the premisses and arguments of feminist theorists from the standpoint of analytic philosophy, without ever hinting at the possibility of assessing the credentials of the assessor. Analytic philosophy is taken to be an unproblematic base from which to assess the claims of feminist theory. She defines her task as 'solving' and 'clarifying' 'women's problems' from a 'philosophical perspective'. Richards claims that her study of these problems is 'mainly a philosophical one', and what she means by this is that her concern is not so much with 'factual matters' or 'matters of fact' but with techniques of reasoning. In the Introduction to *The Sceptical Feminist*, Richards writes that philosophical questions

> can be classified roughly as those whose solution has nothing to do with empirical matters, but depend on reasoning; on techniques like finding contradictions, showing what follows from what, exposing ambiguities, working out presuppositions, clarifying confusions, and so on.[8]

Her methodology then, is to use such philosophical techniques in order to work out the 'general principles' of justice and to apply these principles to the specific case of women. This is confirmed by the organization of the book. The first four chapters are on reason, nature, freedom and justice and they supply the 'grid' through which 'women's problems' will be addressed in the next five chapters, which concern femininity, women's work, sexuality, fertility and motherhood. The clarity of her treatment of these issues is commendable, but such clarity comes at a high price.

All she is entitled to do within the bounds of this method is to address the relatively superficial question of women's access to justice, freedom and rationality within an already constructed paradigm of what it is to be just, free or rational. Richards does not tackle the question of deep bias in knowledge-construction at all.

The limitations of her approach are in large part the limitations of the analytic conception of philosophy. Paradoxically, for one who as we shall see below considers domestic work a very low grade activity, philosophy is conceived as a kind of conceptual house-cleaning, a matter of 'tidying up' our philosophical terms. The techniques of conceptual analysis are considered to be value-free, as indeed are the techniques of empirical enquiry. Since, on this approach, 'feminist' concerns are either matters of fact or (analytic) philosophical matters, it follows that questions of value are excluded altogether. Perhaps Richards's approach serves above all to demonstrate the barrenness of the analytic method within the field of social and political enquiry. It is in any case a highly contentious claim that questions of value are excluded from the domain of philosophical analysis.[9] So long as the historical and cultural construction of our conceptual schema is not questioned, we will remain blind to the political nature of much of that conceptualization. Richards's treatment of the low value and status accorded to women's work in the private sphere is a case in point.

Richards holds that the type of work women traditionally perform or are especially associated with (for example, nursing, teaching) is likely to be socially downgraded and judged to be of little value. She quotes from the studies of Margaret Mead in this context:

> Men may cook or weave or dress dolls or hunt humming birds, but if such activities are appropriate occupations of men, then the whole society, men and women alike, votes them as important. When the same occupations are performed by women, they are regarded as less important.[10]

According to Richards, whether we can count instances of this kind as cases of genuine discrimination will depend on the response to two questions: 'ought women's work be highly valued?' and 'is it possible for women's work to be highly valued?'[11] Richards argues for a negative response to both questions.

She states that when a particular sort of activity is highly valued then to do well at that sort of activity earns one status. In this way she institutes a rather narrow criterion for judging which sorts of activities are highly valued by noting which sorts of activities attract status. As she defines status as restricted to those activities that have high social visibility, it is a necessary consequence of her view that women's work in the private sphere – precisely because of its privacy – cannot possibly attract status. As she sees it, 'The only way status can appear is in publicly observable things,' and for women this is limited to 'the quality of husband you have managed to catch'.[12] Having defined value in terms of 'publicly observable criteria for success such as promotion and titles and salary',[13] she then informs us that 'This *fact* about the low status of women's work has nothing to do with social *values*.'[14]

Richards is right to identify the privacy and isolation of women's domestic work as a major factor in its low status. However, she is wrong to reduce the issue of value to one of status. She makes a further, unjustified, move when she defines status as *necessarily* concerned with empirically observable or measurable things such as public recognition and financial reward. That status is discerned in these ways and that the value of an activity is often determined by the status of that activity, in our present culture, has everything to do with social *values*. Moreover, it is these values which inform the (social) fact that women's work has a low status. Richards' judgement that it is impossible for women's work to be highly valued cannot be traced to the impossibility of valuing it but rather to the impossibility of it counting as valuable work *within the terms* in which Richards has defined valuable work. Again, Richards is far too willing to accept, as unproblematic fact, that which should be treated as a *social* fact, which embodies social *value*.

Richards believes that even if it were possible to value women's work highly, we *ought not*, since it is undeserving of our value. She claims that 'women's work is of low status not only because of its privacy, but also because of the inherent mediocrity of most of the work.'[15]

Her line of reasoning here is important. She began this chapter by supporting a view of Mead's, that it is not always the type of work that women do that is undervalued but rather it is because women do it that it is undervalued. Whilst Richards agrees that some sorts of work which women are especially associated with, such as nursing and teaching, are undervalued (rather than of low value), she does not see domestic work and childrearing as cases in point. These aspects of (traditional) women's work are not very highly valued because they are *objectively* rather than *conventionally* of low value.[16] She argues that female-dominated occupations, which are undervalued, may be so as the result of this primary association between women and domestic work. Her implicit view then is that there is an *objective* fact, the low value of domestic work, which underpins a conventional value-judgement concerning female-dominated occupations. But why should we follow Richards in thinking that domestic work or childrearing are inherently mediocre activities? The low value and status attached to such work seems itself inescapably a matter of convention.

Another example from *The Sceptical Feminist* shows a similar lack of critical awareness. It was mentioned at the beginning of this chapter that Richards sees herself as a theorist who first 'gets the facts straight' and then decides, having determined the relevant issues of value, how to deal with these facts. The fact/value dichotomy may be seen to be at work in her distinction between *substantial* justice and *formal* justice. She defines substantial justice as a matter of having just laws and formal justice as the impartial and consistent application of laws (which may be just or unjust). Substantial justice, she treats as *objective*, formal justice as *conventional*. Here it is again important to note that Richards is following her earlier formula of working out the general principles first and then applying them to what she calls women's problems. That is, we first work out what we consider substantial justice to be and then measure, alongside it, the formal justice to which women are entitled.

Richards borrows heavily from John Rawls's *A Theory of Justice*[17] in her articulation of the general principles of substantial justice. Feminists have argued that Rawls's theory suffers from a marked sex-blindness which limits what can be said about the specific situation of women within the parameters of his theory. Richards takes no account of such criticisms. Rather, by taking the feminist case and recasting it in the language of *A*

Theory of Justice she *necessarily* misses the depth of the feminist critique against the social and legal treatment of women.

Although the details of Rawls's theory are not relevant here, it is necessary to make some comments on his work since Richards takes his view as adequate to supply the appropriate 'general principles' which will be applied to women's problems. Rawls develops his theory of justice against the background of what he calls the 'original position'. The members of a society formulate their laws and rules under a 'veil of ignorance' concerning their place in society: they have no knowledge of their mental or physical powers, of their life plans or priorities, or of what their status will be in society. By this means he hopes to eliminate the effects of self-interest on agreement concerning what a just society should be like. Given that people do not know how they will be placed within that society, it is in everyone's interest to ensure that the worst-off person is as well off as possible.

In the development of these general principles Rawls makes several assumptions that are unsatisfactory from a feminist perspective. The first and most obvious problem with his approach is that the basic civil unit is implicitly male. Rawls duplicates the assumption of liberal theory that the basic civil unit is a head of a household. Of course there is no necessary reason why a head of a household should be a male person. Contingently, however, it is the case that in our socio-economic structure it is men who have the greatest access to the public sphere and the greatest mobility between the private and the public spheres. Therefore, it is men who are most likely to be heads of households. Secondly, the 'veil of ignorance' takes for granted that it is possible for an individual to take up a 'neutral perspective'. In other words, the subjects of Rawls's original position are conceived as disembodied and interchangeable beings. He thus duplicates the most serious problems of the liberal perspective that I criticized in an earlier chapter.

Moller Okin and others have pointed out that these problems present serious flaws in Rawls's theory.[18] However, in the context of Richards's use of Rawls to address issues of sexual justice, the results are disastrous. The effect of Rawls's injunction to 'think of the parties as heads of families' is quite contrary to what he hoped to achieve, which was 'to see that the interests of all are looked after'.[19] It is not at all clear how the interests of wives/mothers are 'looked after' on this scheme. Rather, what it achieves is the dismissal of familial and conjugal relations as appropriate subjects for political or legal analysis. As Okin states 'the "head of family" assumption, far from being neutral or innocent, has the effect of banishing a large sphere of human life (i.e. the family) – and a particularly large sphere of most women's lives – from the scope of the theory.'[20] It is a theory that has next to nothing to say about the specific issue of sexual justice, the very issue which Richards purportedly seeks to address. Richards can address issues of justice between men and women, *only in so far as* men and women are conceived as neutral, interchangeable and competing agents in the public sphere. Once again, the specifically feminist point, that so-called *personal* or *private* relations between men and women are also *political* and *economic* relations, is obscured.

Rawls's two assumptions referred to above actually collude to render women, *qua* wives, mothers, and domestic workers, invisible as agents or recipients of legal and moral relations. The private sphere tacitly takes on the mantle of 'natural' relations as opposed to artificial or socio-political ones. This point bears directly on Richards's methodological commitments. Her criticism, in the introduction to her book, that 'feminism often suffers from staying too close to women, and not looking enough at the general principles which have to be worked out and then applied to women's problems'[21] can be interpreted as a confusion, on her part, concerning the feminist project. It is an instance of the conflation mentioned earlier concerning the two levels on which feminist critique operates. Richards consistently discerns only the first level. She seems unable to question the very foundations and legitimacy of the theoretical tools she herself uses.

This necessarily brief account of the conceptual difficulties of using Rawls is intended to illustrate just where Richards's approach goes wrong. From *where* do these general principles issue? From whose perspective, which history, what culture, do they emanate? Rawls's general principles are not value-free. They are permeated with values and liberal assumptions that have developed in a historical context of male privilege. What Richards fails to appreciate is that it is by concentrating on the specificity of women's situations and developing what has been named a 'woman-centred' perspective, that the masculine bias inherent in our 'general principles' has become visible. Whilst there are several difficulties with this 'woman-centred' perspective, some of which I will address in the latter half of this chapter, it has nevertheless been a necessary and indispensable phase in feminist theorizing. Richards's use of Rawls's theory undoes this work by rendering women's traditional roles invisible in the political domain.

2 Back to the Future?

It has already been noted that McMillan shares several of Richards's assumptions concerning feminist theory. However, unlike Richards, McMillan takes a critical stance toward ways of conceptualizing human life. She does this from a Wittgensteinian and Winchean perspective, where the *context* of human action is taken to be crucial to understanding the *meaning* of that action. She has some positive critical contributions to make to feminist theory in relation to the question of what makes human life distinctively human. McMillan rightly chastises feminists such as de Beauvoir and Firestone for passively accepting the reason/emotion dichotomy and the traditional association of masculine activity with reason and feminine activity with emotion. McMillan reasons that 'feminists share with their antagonists views about the nature of rationality and about the relation between reason and personhood that are plagued with difficulties.'[22] Whilst her criticisms of de Beauvoir and Firestone are generally fair, McMillan overstates her case by generalizing her specific objections to these particular theorists to *all* feminists.

McMillan acknowledges the low value accorded to women's traditional roles, whilst insisting that this value is not an absolute but a social value which must be challenged. Her argument is that men and women, and their relation to culture and nature, are necessarily different but equally valuable and socially necessary. There is no justification for accepting the superior value accorded to scientific knowledge and those achievements and activities that are traditionally masculine. In fact, in so far as de Beauvoir and Firestone accept the superior value of these activities, they are as sexist as their antagonists. McMillan offers some interesting and important arguments in this context. Contrary to Richards' argument concerning domestic work, McMillan offers a convincing argument against the claim that technical reason involves an excellence lacking in the more practical reason involved in, say, running a household or raising a child.[23]

However McMillan argues for the reappraisal of the contributions of women to culture in a way that is uncritical of the *production* of differential values for traditional male and female roles, or of the way in which these values are embedded in and reproduced by social institutions and practices. She argues for the 'different but equally valuable and necessary' view of sexual difference in a manner that does not adequately address the construction of women as intuitive, nurturing and close to nature. I will argue below that her failure to address the organization of the sexes, and their roles, around the public/private distinction renders her plea for the reappraisal of the female role practically vacuous.

McMillan is keen to stress the social context of actions or behaviours in the task of deciphering their meaning and value. However, she does not seem to note that, historically, our political and economic arrangements have constructed and continue to perpetuate conditions of life that are antithetical to women's social, political and economic possibilities. In this she lags far behind her principal critical targets: de Beauvoir and Firestone. For all their problems, they opened up several avenues of enquiry that have proved fruitful for later feminists. They attempted to address both woman as a historical product *and* the future possibilities for woman given this history. McMillan has virtually nothing to say on either question, preferring to take an ahistorical and essentialist line on questions of human nature. Like Richards, she seems unable to discern that feminist theorists have worked, and continue to work, on these two fronts: an analysis of what women presently are and an exploration of their future possibilities. McMillan's startling criticisms of feminist objections to socialization practices provide examples of her confusion.

McMillan boldly asserts that 'at least one aim of feminism is the *abolition* of socialisation.'[24] Feminists have argued that much of what we take to be human nature is in fact the result not of nature or biology but of social training and practices. They have argued that many of these practices are oppressive and stultifying, resulting in the narrowing of women's possibilities. Moreover, many women are placed in roles that are contradictory and confusing, making it difficult for them to live up to the ideals of femininity that society holds up to them. McMillan does not understand these arguments to be directed at *particular* social practices but rather at *all* socialization practices. Clearly, this would be an absurd position to hold, as she has little trouble demonstrating.

It is perhaps significant that neither A. Oakley's *Sex, Gender and Society* (1972) nor J. Mitchell's *Psychoanalysis and Feminism* (1974) – two texts crucial to the development of feminist understandings of socialization – appear in McMillan's bibliography. Yet, she has no compunction in offering the highly generalized statement that 'feminists assert, *without argument*, that our sex conventions are not directly related to [the facts of birth and death] at all'!'[25] In fact, what many feminists do not accept is the highly contentious view of the relation between 'natural facts' and 'social conventions' to which McMillan, following Winch, subscribes.

Her central argument is that feminists do not understand the relation between nature or biological facts and the social conventions which are founded upon them. At this point it is necessary to examine McMillan's understanding of the Winchean position before returning to criticize her view of the relation between nature and convention. In *The Idea of a Social Science* Winch, according to McMillan, argues that:

> the meaning of a word is to be found in its use. Since the use of a word presupposes a social context, it is always there that we have to look for clarification of its meaning. And since the rules governing the use of a word may differ from context to context, it is only when we are quite clear *which rules or criteria govern certain assertions* that we can be sure that we have understood what is being said. This means that the kind of puzzlement we feel, for example, about whether there is a female nature, or what someone means by appealing to such a conception, will be resolved satisfactorily only by

elucidating the *internal relations*, if there are any, that obtain between the variety of things that we call feminine.[26]

This method, when applied to the difficult problem of the relation between biological fact and social convention, yields the insight that:

> I do not want to say – as do feminists – that the absence of a causal relation between biological facts and behaviour means that the general natural or biological realities of human life are irrelevant to this discussion. Rather, the point is that if we want to understand how such facts affect our lives, what we require is not a study in biochemistry but an account of *the internal relations between our sexual conventions and the natural facts of which they aim to make sense*. Indeed much of the difficulty with the way in which feminists think of our notions of femininity stems, crucially, from the fact *they fail to relate our beliefs about sex differences to the biological realities* of the fact that human life begins with *birth* and that, for women, sex is inextricably bound up with procreation.[27]

Quite apart from the inaccuracy of her charge against feminists there are serious problems with this view of the internal relations between natural facts and social or sexual conventions. The most an investigation of this sort would yield is an understanding of the *specific* sense that a *particular* culture makes of its form of life. And even then, if we question the notion of the homogeneity of any particular culture, this method will only yield the *dominant* understanding of this relation. Any culture is an heterogeneous conglomeration of varying, and often inconsistent or contradictory, ideas about the relation between social conventions and 'facts of nature'. If this were not the case it would be very difficult to see how the question of alternative views of this relation could exist at all. Social conventions, and the rationalizations that support them, are much more dynamic than McMillan's static account allows. The historical dynamism of our understandings of what are taken to be *necessary* features and what are taken to be artificial or *conventional* features of human life is precisely what allows the positing of different ways of coping with, or organizing, these 'facts of life'. This is precisely what many feminist theorists, from Wollstonecraft to the present day, have attempted to do: offer alternative ways of understanding the relation between biology and social life and at the same time posit possible options for organizing social life differently.

McMillan then goes on to confuse a method for *understanding* social life with a method of *justifying* social practices. Certainly, most feminists would be interested in any method which purports to understand social life, but for them such understanding, rather than justifying social conventions, would offer an analysis of how patriarchy functions in this or that culture. It is difficult to see how the social methodology employed by McMillan, at least from her account of it, could ever yield a *politically* informed analysis. As is frequently the case when social theorists turn to an analysis of *sexual* conventions, these conventions are deemed to have a *natural* rather than a *political* basis. McMillan, like other philosophers considered thus far, treats women's roles in functional terms only. The roles that women perform in the private sphere are assumed to be an inevitable outcome of the natural functioning of female biology. Little or no importance is accorded to the effects of social and political institutions on human bodies and their capacities. McMillan, not surprisingly, is in complete agreement with Rousseau concerning the natural rather than political basis of our sexual conventions.[28] Essentially it is the strong humanism of McMillan's account that commits her to the fundamentally static grid provided by the triad: birth, death, sexual relations. Following Vico, she maintains that it is the superimposition of this grid alone upon social practices that provides an understanding of those practices.

We can now begin to make sense of several accusations that McMillan makes against feminists and discern the confusions upon which they are based. Returning to the chapter on socialization, it is now evident, in the light of her understanding of internal relations, how she can claim that 'feminists conflate the notions of authority and power.'[29] This alleged conflation is important in the context of criticizing feminist views on the socialization of children. Authority, on McMillan's understanding, is little more than *legitimate* power and what legitimates certain power relations is their place in the system of rules which govern and constitute meaningful behaviour. This view of power, authority and what constitutes behaviour as meaningful begs all the questions raised in this section. In particular, it begs the political question of the relationship between a *description* and a *justification* of our social practices. Juliet Mitchell, for example, takes psychoanalytic theory to be an accurate description of certain aspects of patriarchal society but not, as some have supposed, a justification for it.[30] It is difficult to see how such a distinction could be maintained on McMillan's view. In the absence of such a distinction it becomes evident that where feminists may see a helpful description of the way in which social beings make sense of their embodiment and their relation to nature, McMillan sees a justification for current practices. This view allows her to posit that 'the differences in the child-rearing roles of men and women are fundamentally and significantly biological.'[31] Likewise, where feminists may make a theoretical distinction between what they take women's biology to be and the way in which that biology is 'lived' in culture,[32] McMillan will miss this distinction and understand feminist attempts to articulate it as 'a sort of rebellion against nature [and] not against patriarchal institutions.'[33] This inability to distinguish between what Adrienne Rich, for example, has called the experience of motherhood as opposed to the institution of motherhood, is tied up with McMillan's lack of attention to the institutional or political nature of the public/private distinction. It is as if she sees the affairs of the private sphere to be the natural or inevitable outcome of the 'inescapable biological facts' of human existence. Yet, the particular form of family life that we take as natural is a fairly recent development[34] and its specific character is bound up with political and economic factors.

McMillan's plea for the revaluing of women's traditional role and for the preservation of this role in our current context is both romantic and unrealistic. Moreover, her conservatism, in the literal sense, leads her into a narrow and oppressive prescriptivism that does not sit easily with other values which she professes. For example, she asserts that:

> A young boy will hardly have to consider limits placed on his working life by pregnancy and the need to suckle infants, whereas a girl needs to be made to face squarely the physical restrictions that pregnancy and children will impose on her possible range of activities . . . *and to think of her life in relation to these.*[35]

If men do not consider fathering children to be a limitation on their working lives, it seems to me that this has less to do with *biological facts* and much more to do with the way our society organizes the demands of (paid) work and the demands of childcare such that the performance of both by the same individual entails spatial, temporal and emotional contradictions. The feminist point is not, of course, to abolish the family or to abolish socialization (whatever that could mean). Rather, it is critically and constructively to examine alternative ways of organizing human life that would allow women, and men, greater flexibility, self-determination and choice in the course of their lives. In exploring these possibilities some feminists have been very careful to distinguish between the family as we know it and the family as it could be. It is the former that is the target for criticism. Rich, for example, in *Of Woman Born: Motherhood as Experience and Institution* (1976) stresses this distinction in the following terms:

> This book is not an attack on the family or on mothering, except as defined and restricted under patriarchy.[36]
>
> . . . the patriarchal institution of motherhood is not the 'human condition' any more than rape, prostitution and slavery are.[37]
>
> To destroy the institution is not to abolish motherhood.[38]

What becomes evident from a careful reading of McMillan's text is that it is not so much biological fact which dictates the social roles of the sexes but the values which she often surreptitiously imports into her interpretation of these 'facts'. In her eagerness to assert her values over those of others, she makes several claims that are both morally and intellectually irresponsible. The kind of attitude that she takes to be appropriate to our situation is one which is not even a practical option for most people. The sacredness and dignity of women's role in the private sphere is a view that can only rarely be sustained in the current political and economic context. If followed, her views on the duties of women and mothers – two terms which she constantly collapses[39] – would achieve little more than placing women in impossibly contradictory positions.

Whilst McMillan does offer a cogent critique of the many drawbacks to the so-called liberation of women from their bodies,[40] she is quite wrong to locate feminism as the *cause* of this false liberation. Many feminists themselves had already written in detail on these drawbacks.[41] By some mysterious process of reasoning McMillan identifies feminism as responsible for the very conditions that feminists seek to ameliorate.[42]

McMillan has no suggestions for ways of empowering women to cope with modern life that do not assume marriage to an ideally well-informed, reasonable man who is willing to agree that 'the sexual act is, fundamentally and potentially, a procreative one' and 'People who do not wish to accept this fact and the responsibility it entails should not have sex.'[43] Moreover, he must be financially and emotionally capable and willing to support his wife and family. When one considers that the small percentage of the male population *capable* of doing this will be further depleted by the condition of *willingness*, one begins to question the practical relevance of McMillan's view. She assumes an ethics of conjugal relations, heavily spiced with Catholicism, which from an economic perspective alone is anachronistic.

Moreover, McMillan's defence of the private sphere, and women's traditional role within it,[44] colludes in the maintenance of the alienated public sphere which she elsewhere[45] decries. It is often only the recuperation experienced in the private sphere that makes the brutality of the public sphere bearable at all. This could be seen either as an argument for retaining the private sphere or as another reason for abolishing it. If the private sphere were not available as a 'safety valve' for the tensions and impersonality of the public sphere, perhaps the result would be improved conditions and relations in the latter. Along with Rousseau, she sees the familial sphere, with women at its centre, as a timeless, ahistorical enclave of nature. And like Rousseau, she wishes to entrust to women the impossible task of preserving the family, love and so-called natural relations from the intrusions of technology and the depersonalization this entails. For many feminists, this is tantamount to entrusting women with the preservation of patriarchy itself. This is the very task that Daly, whose work I will discuss at the end of this chapter, exhorts women to repudiate.

3 The Language, Thought and Reality Thesis

As we have seen in the first part of this chapter, Richards maintains that language, used properly, is a *neutral* vehicle for reasoning about matters of fact. This applies particularly to philosophical language, which on her view is the paradigm of rigorous and unambiguous language use. Dale Spender, by contrast, rejects the supposed sexual neutrality of language, or indeed of logic and matters of fact. On her view, logic, facts and modes of conceptualization are all caught in what she calls 'the language trap', and in a patriarchal society this trap will be one which consistently favours men and denigrates women. Her argument is that men have 'controlled the language' and that 'it works in their favour.'[46]

Spender utilizes the work of Benjamin Whorf, who argued that language, thought and reality are inextricably bound together.[47] His thesis, roughly, is that the language we use determines the limits of what can be thought and constructs the reality we inhabit. Our perceptions of both the natural and the social world are determined by and dependent on the language we use. Spender puts it this way:

> Human beings cannot impartially describe the universe because in order to describe it they must first have a classification system. But, paradoxically, once they have that classification system, once they have a language, *they can see only certain arbitrary things.*[48]

The obvious implication of this view, which Whorf developed in conjunction with his study of the Hopi Indian language, is that radically different languages give rise to radically different thought processes and perceptual experiences. Quite different languages may construct realities which do not overlap significantly, one with the other, making translation from one to the other difficult, if not impossible.

There are several problems with this view, some of which I will treat below. These problems, however, should not be allowed to eclipse the positive contributions made by Spender's analysis of language. One of the most important aspects of her work is the understanding which she brings to bear on the issue of the *depth* of the conceptual bias against women. Spender is on strongest ground when she is arguing for what I will call the weak thesis. This is that *particular* uses of language often involve an implicit or explicit bias against women. This problem has become particularly evident in the humanities, especially since women have entered those disciplines in significant numbers.

In the chapter entitled 'The Politics of Naming', Spender considers John Archer's findings concerning the biased way in which psychologists investigate sex differences. Her comments provide an illuminating example of the more critical stance she adopts towards the fact/value distinction. Archer offers the example of an experiment that was designed to test if there were sex differences in the way in which subjects perceived a stimulus in a circumscribed field. In Spender's words, 'subjects could either *separate* the stimulus (an embedded figure) from the surrounding field or else they could see the *whole*, they could see the stimulus as part of the surrounding field.'[49] The experiment yielded the result that men were more likely to perceive the stimulus in the former and women in the latter manner. The (male) researcher labelled this difference as 'field independence' and 'field dependence', respectively. Spender argues that this process of naming is inherently *political*. The researcher has encoded his bias by, implicitly, assigning the *positive* value (independence) to the male subjects and the *negative* value (dependence) to the female subjects. Spender suggests that an alternative way of naming the difference, admittedly no less political, would be to call the male response 'context blind' and the female response 'context aware'. This would reverse the positive and negative connotations put on this sex difference by the original researcher. This is an important point and one which holds good in many different contexts.

Consider the contrast between Richards' approach to 'women's problems' and the approach suggested by Spender's views. One of the arguments Richards offers in favour of varying the requirements for females for admission to professional careers is that by this means we will improve the social position of women. She argues that this is *not* discrimination since we are selecting our candidates for reasons that include the improvement of women's lot. This argument needs to be quoted in full:

> We want good doctors, certainly, but at the same time we want to encourage people to think of women as doctors. *If, as a matter of fact, we think that the best way to achieve this is to have a good many successful women doctors, we may consider making rules which allow women to become a doctor with slightly lower medical qualifications than a man. But this does not offend against the principle that there should be no discrimination in selection procedures, because we are still concerned to choose the best people for the job which needs doing.* It is just that the nature of the work to be done has changed, so that different people become suitable for it. We now want, for example, good doctors who *also* advance the position of women. As long as lowering the medical qualifications for women was causally relevant to the end achieved, it would be justified.[50]

Richards does not question the *criterion of selection* for the best or most competent applicant, she merely suggests *lowering* it in the case of women. I see no reason why Richards favours the lowering of the criterion of selection for women rather than suggesting the criterion itself be *changed*. If we take into account the importance of kindness, communication skills and respect for others in the selection of our doctors – traits which, as Richards suggests herself, many doctors, unfortunately, currently lack[51] – we may find that female applicants, generally, will fare better if these (stereotypically feminine) qualities are part of the selection procedure. This, however, does involve *questioning* existing criteria, something which Richards is loath to do. She seems to miss the point, made so well by Spender, that selection criteria are themselves not value-free. Adding values, which may be particularly important to many women, does not turn a *neutral* criterion into a value-laden one – it merely *adds* further values.

For Spender, to be human is to be bound by a particular language and by particular conceptual schema and so be always *inside* a system of thought, unable to think or speak from an ideally neutral standpoint. This is, for her what it *is* to be a language user. Thought and reality itself are bound to and limited by the language which we use. She adds a further dimension to the language, thought and reality thesis by adding what she calls a 'linguistic translation' of the work of two anthropologists: Edwin Ardner and Shirley Ardner. They argued that the credibility of much anthropological discourse is questionable since many anthropologists consult only men in their field work. This results in a partial view of the particular society under study, since only half of its inhabitants have been consulted concerning their social rules, customs and meanings. Edwin Ardner introduced the terms 'dominant group' and 'muted group' to describe this phenomenon. Men are taken to be the dominant and women the muted group. This terminology was developed for a specific discipline, and in a specific context: that of (predominantly male) anthropologists' study of other cultures. However, Spender introduces it holus-bolus into her discussion of language and this gives rise to several confusions.

Understanding patriarchy as a form of social organization where men are the dominant and women the muted group, Spender ventures that:

> it has been the dominant group – in this case, males – who have created the world, invented the categories, constructed sexism and its justification and developed a language trap that is in their interest,

and, further, that

> The group which has the power to ordain the structure of language, thought and reality has the potential to create a world in which they are the central

figures, while those who are not of their group are peripheral and therefore may be exploited.[52]

This strikes me as a highly simplistic, polarized and unconvincing thesis. It gives rise to problems in Spender's position which undermine those parts of her thesis that are important and sound.

If thought and reality are dependent on language, and if it is men who have produced and controlled language, with women playing the part of mere consumers, then how does the question of distinct male and female realities arise at all? If these realities are dependent upon humanly produced classificatory systems, and in patriarchy this production is restricted to men, then women as consumers of this language should be in perfect agreement with male thought and male-constructed reality.

The dominant/muted hypothesis does little more than posit a theoretical space where women's language may exist (and therefore, female thought processes and female reality). From the perspective of an anthropologist, in the context of his or her own discipline, this 'theoretical space' may make sense. Clearly, it calls for the presence of female anthropologists in the field to study and report on female perceptions of a society, its rules, and so on. However, in the context of a feminist critique of language it is unsatisfactory to posit a noumenal world where women's language, thought and reality exist, but in a muted form. The problem is stated quite clearly, albeit unintentionally, by Spender herself:

> Inherent in this analysis of dominant/muted groups is the assumption that women and men will generate different meanings, that is, *that there is more than one perceptual order*, but that only the 'perceptions' of the dominant group, with their inherently partial nature, are encoded and transmitted.[53]

The obvious problem here is that if we take the Whorf hypothesis seriously, different perceptual orders *necessarily* imply different languages and different thought processes. Yet, in patriarchal society, she argues, it is men who invent language and construct reality. There are two, mutually exclusive, ways out of this paradox: either women have their own language, thought and reality, but it remains hidden (apparently even from women), or the Whorf thesis should be abandoned by Spender as inappropriate to her purposes. If we choose the first option then we are faced with the likely consequence that there are separate male and female realities, and that these realities are perhaps inaccessible to each other. This thesis seems to be easily falsifiable. It involves entertaining the notion that male/female communication is always already foredoomed or the idea that we need to replace male-dominated language, thought and reality with female-dominated language, thought and reality. Neither option seems politically viable or desirable. If we choose the second way out of the paradox, and abandon the Whorf thesis, then the claim that men made language, and the concomitant claim that thought and reality are male, lose their theoretical support. Either way, Spender's strong thesis loses a good deal of its credibility.

The problem seems to be that Spender has *overstated* her case. It is certainly true that, on occasions, women may interpret, perceive or experience the same event in ways that differ radically from men. But this experience may also occur amongst women, between different cultural groups or between people of different political persuasions. To give primacy and privilege to the difference between male and female experiences is not only ahistorical, it also leaves unanalysed one of the most important binary oppositions in our thought processes: that between the terms 'male' and 'female'. Spender does not explore the ways in which this opposition is itself constructed and maintained within particular theories but instead takes it as her starting point. This, in turn, leads her into a theoretical dead end, since she is reduced to maintaining a conspiracy theory, of sorts, to explain men's alleged monopoly on language. This may, in certain circumstances, be quite accurate.[54] However, to locate a conspiracy, on the part of men, as the single source of their domination and control of language is to overestimate both their power and the level of conscious awareness available to any socially or politically oppressive group.[55]

Although Spender occasionally acknowledges the interconnectedness of language revision and socio-political change,[56] at other times she writes as if a voluntary act of the will is sufficient both for men to dominate language and for women to construct a revised language that will better reflect, or make visible, women's reality.[57] The problem here is that there are many, often contradictory or inconsistent, interpretations of social and political reality held contemporaneously by different sections of society. To say this does not require the positing of 'separate realities', let alone separate male and female realities. If this were not the case it would be difficult to explain the conflictual and dynamic nature of our society and the production of new linguistic meanings. Indeed, Spender herself must hold a view something of this kind or her comments on Daly's view of language would make little sense. Quoting Daly, Spender states:

> There is no need for an entirely new set of words in a material sense of new sounds or letters, but rather that 'words which, materially speaking, are identical with the old become new in a semantic context that arises from *qualitatively new experience.*'[58]

The problem remains that if we take Spender's strong language, thought and reality thesis seriously, then 'qualitatively new experiences', that are specifically feminist, must be created *ex nihilo*.

4 Naming the Demons

Gyn/Ecology: The Metaethics of Radical Feminism is written as a journey or voyage of Odyssean proportions, through the 'foreground' of patriarchal culture into the 'background' of 'Self-Identified Spinsters'. This voyage too has its Sirens, its Charybdis and Scylla and the lures of Circe. However, these female goddesses and monsters that Ulysses encountered are aids rather than hindrances to female journeyers. The lures and snares that female voyagers will encounter are quite different in kind to those that confronted Ulysses. For the Spinster spinning through and beyond patriarchal culture, the dangers are the snares and traps of (patriarchal) language, (patriarchal) scholarship and the 'false (patriarchal) self'.[59]

Gyn/Ecology can be read, on one level at least, as an existentialist project or quest for the authentic 'True Self' of women. Daly makes use of much existentialist terminology: the necessity to 'choose' ourselves; the radical freedom that resides in be-ing; the creative movement of transcendence that thrusts us into a future which we are obliged to invent. Her writing is an incitement to women to reconsider past choices and past loyalties and to choose to 'cast themselves into the world' as free subjects.

> For women to reconsider our earlier paternally prescribed tendencies, deceptively misnamed 'decisions', is nothing less than daring to see, name and reach for the stars. It is reclaiming our original movement, our Prehistoric questing power which has been held down by the inner/outer artificial ceilings/sealings of the State of Servitude. De Beauvoir writes that 'life is occupied in both perpetuating itself and in surpassing itself; if all it does is maintain itself, then living is only not dying . . .' This maintenance level of 'only not dying' is what I am calling robotitude. The problem is to get beyond the maintenance level, for 'a life justifies itself only if its effort to perpetuate itself is integrated into its surpassing and if this surpassing has no other limits than those which the subject assigns himself [herself].'[60]

Alongside this use of existentialist terminology is an inventive and transgressive use of religious terminology. Terms such as 'Otherworld', 'exorcise', 'Re-ligious', 'ecstasy' and 'Rebirth' are all invested with new meaning. Daly invents some terms to create new significances (for example, 'fembot', 'gynaesthesia', 'gynography') and recycles other terms, destroying their past significances and investing them with new meaning (for example, 'hag', 'harpy', 'spinster').

The analysis of language is crucial throughout the three sections of *Gyn/Ecology*. Daly warns the voyager that

[i]t is an essential task of feminist metaethics to examine and analyse [this] language, untangling the snarls of sentence structure, unveiling deceptive words, exposing the bag of semantic tricks intended to entrap women.[61]

Daly attempts to expose the violence involved in quite simple linguistic acts.[62] She often has recourse to the etymology of words such as 'glamour' and 'spinster', pointing out that these words originally conveyed a sense of women's power and independence. In her quest to reclaim women's eroded power and autonomy, she reasserts these past meanings and enjoins others to use them in this reinvested, positive sense. Hence, journeyers are named Hags, Spinsters and Harpies, who spin through and then away from patriarchy into an indefinite, but free, future. The seriousness with which Daly treats the act of naming endows it with a power bordering on the magical. The idea that one can control, disarm or destroy one's enemy by naming him is a constant sub-theme in *Gyn/Ecology*. This idea is common in Greek myth and in fairytales (for example, Rumpelstiltskin). 'When we say their names, they – in effect – drop dead.'[63] Having faced, and named, the worst atrocities that our necrophilic culture is capable of, the reader is 'freed' of its disabling force.

Daly's account of our culture is a highly polarized one: women are simplistically presented as biophilic and men as necrophilic. She claims that patriarchal culture is grounded in the death-wish and that 'Woman hating is at the core of necrophilia.'[64] Her analysis leaves itself open to all the accusations of irrational fanaticism that it has often received. She was not unaware of the likelihood of this kind of response. In the introduction to *Gyn/Ecology* she writes, 'This is an extremist book, written in a situation of extremity, written on the edge of a culture that is killing itself and all of sentient life.'[65] In her view, the seriousness of the human situation cannot be exaggerated and the atrocities committed against women, both historically and cross-culturally, represent the epitome of these violent and destructive forces.

Even though Daly claims to be developing a language, an ethics and a world view that is radically different from patriarchal theories, her perspective incorporates much from traditional culture, including many conservative, if not reactionary, elements. As well as 'borrowing' from existentialism and theology, her viewpoint is also fundamentally humanistic. The account she offers of male and female 'nature' is a reversed version of eighteenth-century humanism. The 'True Self' of women occupies the position of ideal type and men play the role of the imperfect, less than human, deviations from the ideal. Significantly, it is man's 'sex' which dooms him to the cycles of brutish violence and to parasitism on women. Although women are frequently represented as victims of male violence in the pages of *Gyn/Ecology*, they are also presented as strong, clear-sighted Amazons whose task it is to save the

planet from destruction by destroying patriarchy. These women are the
'True Selves' whereas women who 'collaborate' with men are 'false selves',
'painted birds', 'daddy's girls' and 'fembots'.

This True Self/false self dichotomy duplicates aspects of the existentialist distinction between authenticity/bad faith. However, unlike de
Beauvoir, Daly seems satisfied with an individualistic rather than a structural analysis of the effects of oppressive social and political relations.
Women who do not accept the gyn/ecological viewpoint are cast as trai-
tors who are 'untrue' to themselves. Evil, by definition, emanates from
men whereas women who commit evil actions are 'false' selves, that is,
selves under the influence of patriarchy. Jean Grimshaw has criticized this
aspect of some forms of radical feminism in the following terms:

> Male behaviour, especially if it is barbaric or brutal, is taken as evidence of
> what male nature is like - and even if men are *not* brutal, they are some-
> times credited with the fundamental desire so to be. But the behaviour of
> women, on the other hand, does not tell us what women are 'really' like.[66]

Grimshaw[67] and Elshtain have both remarked on the similarity between
Daly's derogatory descriptions of male nature and fascistic politics in that
each assumes that their targets (men, Jews) possess a given and unvarying
essence which is identified as the source of the ills of the world. One
problem with this kind of attitude is that it forecloses any possibility of
engagement with the group that is put in the position of the evil other. If
that group is taken to be fundamentally and essentially evil then one can
'justifiably' claim that engagement with them is futile. History has shown,
and unfortunately continues to show us, where this type of reasoning
ends.

It is Daly's assumption of the suffering of all women that allows her to
entertain morally abhorrent views in a book that purports to be concerned with ethics. Elshtain associates this confidence in the purity of
one's speaking position with a naive morality which assumes that those
who suffer have moral purity, simply by virtue of their suffering.[68]

Daly's analysis of the sufferings of women under patriarchy is certainly
the most difficult part of *Gyn/Ecology* to deal with. Not simply because
of the brutality of much of its content but also because of the methodological and theoretical difficulties involved in her levelling of historical
and cross-cultural practices. She describes, and offers an analysis of the
following practices: Indian suttee, Chinese footbinding, African genital
mutilation, European witchburnings, American gynaecology and Nazi
medicine. She takes each of these to be re-enactments of the original
murder of the Goddess. Each practice is cited as evidence of the hatred and
fear that men have for women. Daly insists on the centrality and priority

of misogyny in all forms of violence. In the section on Nazi medicine and concentration camps Daly writes:

> Although their victims – mental patients and Jews – were of both sexes, *all were cast into the victim role modelled on that of the victims of patriarchal gynocide, which is the root and paradigm for genocide.*[69]

and

> The paradigm and context for genocide is trite, everyday, banalized gynocide.[70]

These claims are not only morally wrong, but indefensible in principle. It is not clear what evidence *could* count as verification for the claim that the root of all genocide is gynocide. This claim insults groups, such as Jews, whose specific history and suffering is denied. Further, the claim is a disempowering one for women to entertain since its ahistoricity implies that women are inevitably cast in the role of victim. In fact, it posits women as the 'model' for all victims. This reading can only be maintained on a simplistic and superficial reading of history and cross-cultural differences.

It is in this section of the book that Daly's pre-chosen grid of the four 'methods of the fathers' (erasure, reversal, false polarization, and divide and conquer)[71] seems both forced and arbitrary. She knows which patterns she is looking for and she finds them. For example, women's complicity in some of these practices is unsatisfactorily explained by recourse to the fourth method: token women are used by patriarchy to 'divide and conquer'. This is to refuse the possibility that women can be, or have been, morally responsible agents. Once again, if women behave in an evil manner, it is the false, patriarchal self who is responsible. Evil is given a Manichean status where men are associated with the demonic powers of darkness and the 'True Self' of women with 'life-loving energy'.[72] The (presumably female) reader is enjoined to remember the prehistoric past of the powerful Goddess – she 'who is, and is not yet'[73] – and, by remembering, to bring her into existence. This is a creative remembering. Daly quotes from Wittig's *Les Guérillères*: 'make an effort to remember. Or, failing that, invent.'[74]

But Daly's 'inventions' are not very original. She does not unsettle the fundamental structure of good/bad, light/dark, man/woman. Gyn/ecology merely reverses the traditional associations between these dualisms.[75] This simplistic reversal of traditional dualisms is one of several issues that Gyn/ecology does not adequately address. It is important to recall the sub-title of *Gyn/Ecology: The Metaethics of Radical Feminism*. Daly explains in the introduction that she is not using 'metaethical' in the orthodox sense which she takes to involve 'masturbatory meditations by ethicists upon their own emissions'. Gyn/Ecological metaethics concern 'the mysteries of good and evil'; they 'function to affirm the deep dynamics of female be-ing. It is gynography.'[76] Yet, the kind of ethics the reader is left with may be an ethics *of* the Self or *for* the Self, but it is certainly not an ethics *between* selves.[77] In some sense, Daly does provide an account of what would pass for ethical relations between 'Selves', but these Selves are *necessarily* an extremely specific and small group of women: Spinsters who have made the journey into the background. Leaving these 'authentic' relations aside, however, it would seem that Daly has nothing to say concerning relations, ethical or otherwise, between women and children, women and men or men and children that is not confined to patriarchal atrocities committed against women and children. There is no ethics of *engagement* with others and particularly no ethics of engagement with *different* others. Even the Spinsters do not engage with each other *as* different *others*.

Daly presents the Spinster as an Absolute Subject, centre of her own be-ing, self-sufficient and self-contained, a subject that finds its 'be-ing in the Triple Goddess'.[78] This conception of radical feminist metaethics becomes even more problematic when we consider the True Self/false self dichotomy that runs throughout *Gyn/Ecology*. The True Self is not Daly's way of naming an *achieved* status – as in the existentialist use of 'authenticity' or Nietzsche's understanding of the 'overman' – it is an assumed, pre-given essence. It is the kernel at the heart of (at least, female) being that is revealed once the layers of the 'false self', which 'encase' the True Self, are 'pared away'.[79] Significantly, this True Self seems to be a disembodied self. Here, one is again reminded of the difficulties inherent to the existentialist view of embodiment. As was shown in chapter 3, de Beauvoir's 'modern woman', who achieves authenticity, is one whom repudiates femininity and the female body.

It is noteworthy that Daly's list of atrocities are substantially directed against female *corporeality*, yet corporeality plays little or no part in the background journeying of the Spinsters. After taking great pains to reveal the complex associations between women and corporeality and the way in which female embodiment has been the site of dismemberment, disfigurement and torture, Daly herself seems reluctant to move the female body out of the foreground of patriarchy into the background of feminist metaethics. The True Self seems to be very much a spiritual being and one wonders, in this context, how free Daly is from the effects of her own past, her own religious 'foreground'.

These problems – the essentialist nature of the True Self, the narrowness of radical feminist metaethics, and the apparently disembodied nature of the Spinster – cast doubt on the status of the journey that is *Gyn/Ecology*. Is it a quest for the salvation of the True Soul? Is it a contemporary version of the Augustinian desire to erect 'The City of God[ess]', with men cast in the role of the materialistic Romans? However one responds to these questions, it is clear that *Gyn/Ecology* displays surprising parallels with a genre of medieval religious texts which exhort their readers to disengage from apparent reality in order more fully to recognize the True, that is, spiritual, Reality. Daly's text can be read as recommending a withdrawal from the conditions of contemporary life, including the social, political and ethical relations which govern most women's lives. Daly's ethical stance turns out to be as vacuous as that of McMillan with respect to its relevance to the lives of the vast majority of women.

I began this chapter by stating that the four theorists under consideration each pursue an inadequate strategy in relation to bias against women in philosophy. The criticisms that have been offered of each stance are intended to show that feminist theorists cannot afford to take philosophy as the paradigm of value-free analysis nor to assume that women's experiences can provide a standpoint which is guaranteed to be 'pure' or untainted. This is certainly not to suggest that the work of these theorists is of little value. On the contrary, their efforts either to work toward a feminist perspective or to redeem philosophy have been important in forming the concerns of contemporary feminists. The debate concerning the fact/value distinction continues to be important and the related issue of language and sexual difference is central to much contemporary feminist philosophy.

Perhaps the most important issue to arise from the attempt to create 'woman-centred' theory is the issue of differences *within* the category 'woman'. Contemporary feminism has had to acknowledge that class, race and other differences between women fragment the convenient 'we' of feminist discourses. This fragmentation, in turn, has led to an interrogation of the dualism which is, in many ways, the very foundation of feminism: that of man/woman. Teresa de Lauretis, for example, has maintained that a 'feminist frame of reference . . . cannot be either "man" or "woman", for both of these are constructs of a male-centred discourse.'[80] However, this view maintains a curious allegiance to the biological category 'male' which, it seems to me, is no less problematic than that of 'man'. These issues will be considered in the course of the next three chapters.

5

The Feminist Critique of Philosophy

Over the last four chapters criticisms were offered of some of the ways in which feminist theorists have utilized or rejected philosophical theories. In this chapter I will consider some recent feminist writings which share a deconstructive or critical approach to philosophy. This 'critique of philosophy' differs from other feminist theory in that it does not take 'women's problems' or 'male bias' as its object of study, but rather examines philosophy's history, its binary oppositions and categories, its 'make-up'. In short, this approach studies philosophy as a certain kind of cultural activity, a certain kind of social product. In this way these theorists aim to come to some understanding of how our culture employs and privileges certain categories of thought and what relation these categories have to contemporary understandings of sexual difference. This shift in emphasis concerning the place of philosophy in the development of feminist theory may be seen as effecting a 'quantum leap' whereby feminists no longer feel compelled to view women's situations through existing theories, theories that are antithetical to the development of women's socio-political possibilities.[1]

In the first part of this chapter two common responses of feminists to philosophy are presented. The first response rejects philosophy, its values and its concerns. The second accepts the values of philosophy and its methods of analysis and seeks to extend these to women and their situation. I argue that both responses are inadequate to meet the problems I have presented here. The first, because it underestimates the discursive power of philosophy and its categories of thought in the construction of socio-political life; the second because it over-estimates philosophy and its claims to universality and neutrality. The remainder of this chapter is concerned to argue in favour of a third possible response to the relation between feminist theories and philosophical theories.

1 The Dangers of a Woman-centred Philosophy

The first way in which some feminists have responded to philosophy may be characterized as a form of Radical Feminism or theoretical separatism. These feminists present two kinds of arguments. The first is that there is no relation between feminism and philosophy or more generally between feminism and *theory*. Feminism, on this view, is pure *praxis*, the very activity of theorizing being somehow identified with masculinity or maleness. Perhaps the view of Solanas would be appropriate to quote here. She writes:

> The male's inability to relate to anybody or anything makes his life pointless and meaningless (the ultimate male insight is that life is absurd), so he invented philosophy . . . Most men, utterly cowardly, project their inherent weaknesses onto women, label them female weaknesses and believe themselves to have female strengths; most philosophers, not quite so cowardly, face the fact that male lacks exist in men, but still can't face the fact that they exist in men only. So they label the male condition the Human Condition, pose their nothingness problem, which horrifies them, as a philosophical dilemma, thereby giving stature to their animalism, grandiloquently label their nothingness their 'Identity Problem', and proceed to prattle on pompously about the 'Crisis of the Individual', the 'Essence of Being', 'Existence preceding Essence', 'Existential Modes of Being', etc., etc.[2]

These problems are described by Solanas as specifically *male* problems. The female, on her account, exhibits no such perverse relation to her being which she grasps intuitively and without lack. Philosophy, or theory, on this view is a male enterprise, arising out of an inherent inadequacy of the male sex.

The second argument of feminists, still within this first approach, is that the relationship between feminism and philosophy is historically, and *necessarily*, an oppressive one. This group argues that philosophy is, necessarily, a masculine enterprise that owes its existence to the repression or exclusion of femininity and as such it is of no use to feminists or their projects. In fact, philosophy may be seen, on this view, as a dangerous and ensnaring trap.[3] Both Spender and Daly may be taken as representatives of this response. They do not advocate the abandonment of theory or philosophy *per se*, rather they recommend the rejection of *patriarchal* theory and *patriarchal* philosophy in favour of 'woman-centred' theory. What is clear in their accounts of patriarchal scholarship is that they believe that patriarchal scholars were/are motivated by conscious and malicious intentions which they held/hold towards women. I am not arguing for the inverse view: that misogynistic cultures create misogynistic scholars; rather I am arguing against the viability of any such simplistic causal relation. Unfortunately, neither cultures nor people are as conveniently transparent as this relation implies. The tendency of both Daly and Spender to impute oppressive *intentions* to patriarchal theorists is simply naive.[4] M. le Doeuff has made this point well. She writes:

> Whether we like it or not, we are within philosophy, surrounded by masculine-feminine divisions that philosophy has helped to articulate and refine. The problem is to know whether we want to remain there and be dominated by them, or whether we can take up a critical position in relation to them, a position which will necessarily evolve through deciphering the basic philosophical assumptions latent in discourse about women. *The worst metaphysical positions are those which one adopts unconsciously whilst believing or claiming that one is speaking from a position outside philosophy.*[5]

The failure of Daly to recognize the unconscious determinations of our culture's attitudes towards women and femininity creates problems not only for her appraisal of patriarchal scholarship but also for her faith in the 'True Self' of women and the patriarchally uncontaminated theory/practice/life she thinks them capable of producing. There is an assumed purity and an originary element to her descriptions of this 'True Self' that place it outside of history, language and culture. For example, she argues that:

> It is axiomatic for Amazons that all external/internalized influences, such as myths, names, ideologies, social structures, which cut off the flow of the Self's original movement should be pared away.[6]

As was suggested in the last chapter, unless we assume a soul or an essence to being, Daly's 'True Self', the timeless kernel at the centre of women's being, is an empty fiction. Women no less than men, though undoubtedly in a different fashion, are products of culture and cannot coherently claim for themselves an *a priori* purity or absence of contamination by its values, its language or its myths.

Spender's thesis concerning the generation of new, woman-centred, meanings suffers from similar problems. As mentioned in the last chapter, she seems to believe that conscious volition is at work both in the 'male-hold' on language and in the feminist attempt to break this hold. The battle over language is presented by Spender as a battle between the wills of men and women. Concerning men and language she writes:

> it is obvious that those who have the power to make the symbols and their meanings are in a privileged and highly advantageous position. They have, at least, the potential to order the world to suit their own ends, the potential to construct a language, a reality, a body of knowledge in which they are the central figures, the potential to legitimate their own primacy and to create a system of beliefs which is beyond challenge (so that their superiority is 'natural' and 'objectively tested').[7]

The feminist response to this male privilege and power should be as follows:

> We can *choose* to dispense with male views and values and we can generate and make explicit our own: and we can make our views and values *authentic* and *real*.[8]

It is not clear what would give these woman-centred views and values their authentic or real status. Spender's views on language and value involve an implicit assumption which constructs women's perceptions and values as automatically sound. I fail to see the rationale, let alone the justification, for this judgement. The refuge she takes in a pluralistic relativism, where everyone's meanings are valid, for them, only confounds this issue further.[9]

The major source of my disagreement with both these writers is their tendency simultaneously to include and exclude women from (patriarchal) culture, language and values. Women suffer oppression, exploitation and effacement in culture at the same time as they stand apart from culture. That part of female consciousness that is enmeshed in culture is corrupt (viz. Daly's fembots, painted birds, daddy's girls, etc.) but that part that somehow stands apart from culture is the source and guarantee for the authenticity of feminist insight and woman-centred meaning. This false/true dichotomization of women is untenable. It results in the positing of a hierarchy of *types* of women: the oppressed woman who cannot, because she lacks education or opportunity, see through her condition; the complicit woman who chooses not to acknowledge her condition through fear of losing class privilege and having to accept responsibility for her own life; and the authentic woman who recognizes her oppression and chooses to struggle to overcome it. This pattern of describing women was noted in the work of de Beauvoir[10] and is also clearly present in the work of Daly and Spender. The problem is that empirical women rarely, if ever, fit neatly into one or other of these categories and rarely experience their lives as the result of conscious choice. The lived condition of most women tends to be rather more complex than this hierarchy allows. In terms of this first approach then, the response to the perceived relation between feminism and philosophy is to choose feminism – understood either as pure praxis or as uncontaminated theory – *over* philosophy. This approach to philosophy has several problems.

First, it is dependent for its rationale on an unspoken and unexamined proposition that philosophy, as a discipline or an activity, coincides with its past. It assumes that philosophy is and will be what it was. This reification of philosophy misses the point that philosophy is, among other things, a human activity that is *ongoing*. It is a cultural product that, as Marx observed, reflects the values, concerns and power relations of the culture which produces it.[11] The objects of philosophical enquiry typically include such things as human being, its cultural, political and linguistic environment. Given that these are not static entities, the project of philosophy is necessarily open-ended. The conception of philosophy as a system of truths that could, in principle, be complete, true for all time, relies on the correlative claim that nature or ontology and truth or epistemology are static. In that feminists in the first approach accept the picture that philosophy often presents of itself, it allows this dominant characterization free rein. My argument against this first approach towards the question of the relation between feminism and philosophy, then, is that if it is presented as a long-term programme, it is utopian and runs the serious risk of reproducing elsewhere the very relations which it seeks to leave behind. As other feminists[12] have pointed out, one of the most worrying dangers of this approach is the unwitting affirmation, duplication or repetition of past philosophers' descriptions of women. To affirm women's nature as 'naturally' or 'innately' nurturing, sensitive or biophilic is to ignore the ways in which those qualities have been constructed by social, political and discursive practices.

2 Feminism as the 'Completion' of Philosophy

Whereas the first response sees philosophy as antithetical to feminist aims, the second response identifies the problem as lying with the attitudes of particular (male) philosophers rather than with philosophy itself. This response may be typified by the stance of liberal feminists, although it is not limited to them. Feminists in this category agree that, historically, philosophers have had oppressive relations to women (of misogyny, of omission) but that such relations are not a *necessary* feature of philosophy. They argue or assume that philosophy as a discipline and as a method of enquiry is entirely neutral with regard to sex. Researchers adopting this approach view the history of philosophy as male-dominated, but argue that women are presently in a situation of being able to correct this bias. In this case, the relation between feminist theory and philosophy is envisaged as complementary, one in which feminist theory adds to, or 'completes', traditional or existing philosophy, by filling in the 'gaps' in political, moral and social theories. By adding an analysis of the specific social, political and economic experience of women, this approach seeks to transform philosophy from a male-dominated enterprise into a *human* enterprise.

The response of these feminists sees the relation between feminism and philosophy as complementary but short-lived. Implicit in much of their work is a notion of the 'inbuilt obsolescence' of feminism. Eventually, they suppose, it will be unnecessary to retain a specifically feminist perspective. Once the goal of equality is reached, feminism would be redundant. This assumption is particularly well illustrated by Richards's views on sexual equality and sexual justice which were treated in the last chapter. She redefines feminism as being essentially concerned with the elimination of a certain *type* of injustice. Obviously, once this injustice is eliminated the need for a women's movement would be removed. Criticisms of the superficiality of her analysis were offered in chapter 4 and need not be repeated here.

What this approach usually entails is the adoption of a particular philosophical theory as a method of analysis, and then taking 'woman' as the object, as the philosophical problem. This is what Wollstonecraft attempts, using egalitarianism, in *A Vindication of the Rights of Woman*; what J. S. Mill and Taylor attempt, using liberalism; what de Beauvoir attempts, using existentialism, in *The Second Sex*; and, as we will see in the following chapter, what Mitchell attempts to do by employing both psychoanalysis and Marxism, in *Psychoanalysis and Feminism*. It is work done under the rubric of this second approach that epitomizes the dominant relation between feminism and philosophy since Wollstonecraft. We have seen that Wollstonecraft's views on the education of women reveal a theoretical pre-commitment to egalitarianism. She writes that:

> the most perfect education, in my opinion, is such an exercise of the understanding as is best calculated to strengthen the body and form the heart. Or, in other words, to enable the individual to attain such habits of virtue as will render it independent. In fact, it is a farce to call any being virtuous whose virtues do not result from the exercise of its own reason. This was Rousseau's opinion respecting men; I *extend* it to women . . . [13]

So, we see the general outline of the theory employed by these feminists is considered unproblematic. The problem of how these philosophical theories relate to women is located in a particular male theorist's prejudice, in this case Rousseau's poorly controlled sexual appetite.[14] These feminist theorists attempt to subtract the surface sexism of philosophers and include women in the theory on an equal footing with men. The first half of this book has been concerned to show that this project is doomed to failure. Rousseau's texts may well contain many overtly sexist notions, but the simple removal of these does not allow the equitable inclusion of women. His theory of social contract *requires* the privatization of sexual relations, reproduction and domestic work, along with the confinement of women to the role of wife/mother in the private sphere. The role he assigns to women is pivotal to his ideal society.

The failure to question the necessity of women's exclusion from liberal political life places feminists in paradoxical situations. It is crucial to examine the way in which the public and the private spheres are sexually specified and, in particular, to examine the unacknowledged but crucially supporting role that wives/mothers play in the maintenance of the public sphere. Such examination in turn requires a more critical approach to the dichotomies that dominate Western conceptualizations of human life. We need to be much more sceptical of the reason/passion, mind/body, nature/culture splits and their apparent neutrality and universality with regard to sexual difference. We can no longer assume that these categories are descriptions of *human* being. Rather, we must recognize the ways in which both historically and discursively, each half of a single dichotomy has been more closely associated with one sex than with the other.

There is a marked lack of reciprocity in philosophical accounts of the complementarity between male and female human being. It is woman who, conceptually and literally, acts as the 'bridge' for man between nature and culture, the mind and the body, the private and the public spheres. Whilst she acts as bridge, she herself cannot cross from nature to culture, from body to mind or from private to public. Or, at least, she cannot enjoy both sides of the dichotomy since there is no one, and no concept, to act as her bridge. This problem is partly what is at stake when feminists point out that notions of sexual equality often involve little more than women 'becoming-men' or mimicking men. This problem was evident in the discussion of Richards's use of Rawls's *A Theory of Justice*. Women *qua* wives, mothers and daughters – that is, women in their relations to men – are not offered any protection or justice from the liberal state. The justice they are entitled to is limited to the justice that 'anyone' – meaning any (male) citizen – is entitled to in the public or civic sphere of employment, government, and so on.

Richards's blindness to the contradictions and tensions present to women in their occupation of both the private and public spheres results in her political and ethical neglect of women *qua* mothers, wives and daughters. They are simply not visible in her account of sexual justice.

This invisibility is directly related to the way the above-mentioned dichotomies operate in discussions of sexual difference. Women most often emerge from these analyses as less than human, as bound to their bodies and the exigencies of reproduction, as incapable of a certain kind of transcendence or reason that marks the *truly* human individual. Clearly, the dichotomies which dominate philosophical thinking are not sexually neutral but are deeply implicated in the politics of sexual difference. It is this realization that constitutes the 'quantum leap' in feminist theorizing. It allows a quite different, and more productive, relation to be posited between feminist theories and philosophical theories.

3 The Critique of Philosophy

Whereas feminists who adopt the 'woman-centred' approach argue that women should ignore or avoid philosophical tradition, those who adopt the critique of philosophy approach argue that this tradition must be confronted. As it is a tradition that has helped form our conceptions of masculinity and femininity, to affirm the value of femininity or female experience without analysing the historical construction of this experience is to invite failure and repetition. It is the dichotomies of philosophical thought that have been especially targeted for feminist scrutiny.

Dichotomous categories of thought can be traced to the beginnings of philosophy in ancient Greece. The earliest records we have, from the Ionians, show a table of dichotomous distinctions: good/bad, light/dark, unity/plurality, limited/unlimited and male/female. An important point to note about these distinctions is the associations at work between the left-and right-hand sides of these dichotomies. Maleness is associated with good, light, unity and limitation, all of which have positive connotations. Conversely, femaleness is associated with the negative, right-hand side of these distinctions. Even in the modern period, in the work of Descartes, for example, dichotomies dominate philosophical reflections on the world, human knowledge and human nature. Descartes sought to explain all that exists in terms of one or other of two substances: mind and matter. These dichotomies may be presented by philosophers as logical or theoretical tools, as useful or effective ways of dividing up and understanding the world. Alternatively, they may be seen as neutral, objective or true descriptions of actual divisions in the world, as was the case with Descartes.

The claim here is *not* that dichotomous thought is bad or oppressive *per se*, but rather that it can covertly promote social and political values by presenting a conceptual division as if it were a factual or natural division. Nancy Jay in 'Gender and Dichotomy'[15] offers an excellent analysis of the way in which social and political values may be contained in dichotomies that present themselves as objective distinctions. Take the mind/body distinction as an example: it presents itself as a self-evident distinction, there is nothing to suggest that mind and body are given unequal value and each seems as if it is defined interdependently. However, a close examination of the way these terms function in, say, the philosophy of Descartes, shows that mind is given a positive, and body a negative, value. What appears to be a distinction between A (mind) and B (body), in fact, takes the form of A (mind) and Not-A (body). When we understand the actual functioning of an apparently neutral distinction, the values and the meanings implicit within it become accessible to scrutiny. In this case the term occupying the position A has a primacy and a privilege in relation to defining its partner.

In this way a dichotomy may function to divide a continuous field of differences (A,B,C,D) into an exclusive opposition with one term being singled out to define all the rest: A defines the entire field of Not-A. A is here defined in positive terms, as possessing x,y,z, properties whereas its 'opposite' is negatively defined. Not-A becomes defined by the fact that it *lacks* the properties x,y,z, rather than being defined in its own right. Not-A becomes the privation or absence of A: the fact that it is Not-A is what defines it rather than the fact that it is B. Moreover, as Jay points out, dichotomous thought is structured such that there is an 'infinitation of the negative', the Not-A. What she is referring to here is that because it is only the category A that is positively defined, the category of Not-A can have a potentially infinite number of entities fall under it. Returning to our example, if A is mind then, harking back to Descartes's ontology, Not-A, the field of bodies, includes not only human bodies but also celestial bodies, animal bodies, plants, rocks, and so on, in fact virtually everything that is not-mind. The privileging of A in defining its partner, Not-A, involves a certain lack of coherence in the character of Not-A, or, as Jay puts it, Not-A has no *internal* boundaries.

If Jay's central thesis is correct then the use of dichotomies cannot always be understood as simply a neutral way of dividing up the world into categories. Rather, dichotomies may contain a set of implicit assumptions that assign a prominence and a dominant value to the term in the position of A at the expense of Not-A. This is crucially important in the context of feminist critiques of philosophy, given the predominance of dichotomous thought in that discipline and its tendency to *sexualize* the two sides of any given dichotomy. Jay remarks:

> Hidden, taken for granted, A/Not-A distinctions are dangerous and, because of their peculiar affinity with gender distinctions, it seems important for feminist theory to be systematic in recognizing them.[16]

An examination of the case of the male/female distinction in the history of Western thought, and especially in philosophy, shows that although men and women are different (say A and B) they are commonly defined, openly or implicitly, in a dichotomous fashion.

Jay notes the way in which, in all known cultures, there are ceremonies or rituals whereby (especially male) children make their entry into the community of adolescent males or females. This ceremony is thought to serve two primary purposes: the child is symbolically, or actually, separated from the mother by joining him or her to non-familial structures or social institutions; and through this process the child gains a specific sexual identity and a knowledge of sex-appropriate behaviour. That this ceremony is often exclusively male is telling in itself. It is often only the male child who is publicly defined and acknowledged as male – the female taking on her identity almost by default, that is, by being not-male. There are strong resonances of this structure in Freud's theory of the Oedipus complex, as we will see in the next chapter.

Chodorow[17] too, has remarked on the definitive break that the male child has with the mother compared with the continuity of identity experienced by the female child. Clearly then, this pattern is not peculiar to tribal societies. Our culture exhibits its own forms of sexual initiation. These forms are reflected in our linguistic and conceptual history. Aristotle, for example, regarded women as 'deformed men'. From ancient Greece to our own time women have been defined not so much in terms of any positive qualities that they possess but rather in terms of the male qualities that they lack. For the Greeks it was lesser reason; for others it was lesser strength; for Freud women lack (or have only an atrophied) penis. The important feature to note is that there is a history of women being defined only in terms relative to men, who are taken as the norm, the standard or the primary term. This structure mirrors the structure of dichotomy as outlined by Jay. Moreover it is a structure that cannot be explained simply in terms of conscious or unconscious male prejudice or sexism. It is typical of a form of thought that has been termed phallocentric. A more detailed analysis of phallocentrism will be offered in the following chapter where the work of Luce Irigaray, including her use of deconstruction, will be discussed. It is sufficient to note here that phallocentrism operates by way of dichotomous thought, where one central term defines all others only in terms relative to itself.

A recent example of feminist critique which confirms the foregoing analysis of the way dichotomies function in the history of Western philosophy is Genevieve Lloyd's The Man of Reason: 'Male' and 'Female' in Western Philosophy.[18] Lloyd's careful analysis of the history of conceptions of reason aims to demonstrate that 'the maleness of the Man of Reason . . . is no superficial linguistic bias.'[19] Rather, she argues, the latent conceptual connections between reason, masculinity, truth and the intellect, on one hand, and sense, femininity, error and emotion, on the other, are so entrenched and pervasive in the history of philosophy that they virtually prohibit women from reason. Women have experienced, and often still do experience, practical limits to their participation in reason: such things as lack of access to institutions, illiteracy, forced confinement to the domestic sphere, and so on. Lloyd argues that there are also *discursive* barriers between reason and femininity.

Two major theses of her work are important here: first, she argues that reason has defined itself in opposition to femininity; and second, femininity as a discursive category, and as lived by women, is constituted, at least partly, by this exclusion. This last claim is of obvious importance to the viability of the claims of a woman-centred perspective. If this perspective is partly constituted by women's exclusion from male-defined norms, then in what sense could it be said to be 'authentic' or 'real'?[20] Lloyd aims to concentrate mainly on conceptions of reason but her general analysis can be made to hold good in relation to other distinctions important in political and ethical philosophy. In what follows it will be argued that an analysis of the nature/culture and public/private dichotomies reveals a similar pattern to the one deciphered above. Women's supposed close association with nature and the private sphere will be shown to be, at least partly, an effect of the way these distinctions are dichotomously conceived.

Eighteenth-century political philosophy furnishes an interesting series of constructions of nature and the supposed affinity that women and the family have with it. In *Emile*, for example, Rousseau writes that 'Natural relations remain the same throughout the centuries.'[21] This sentiment sits very uneasily in the broad thesis of *Emile* which purports to be concerned with the inevitable and corrupting alterations to nature and natural relations that accompany a highly developed civilization. In order to penetrate the meaning of this sentence we must understand that for Rousseau it is only by the rational and artificial *reconstruction* of nature that the uneasy relations between nature and culture, the man and the citizen, the family and the state, can be harmonized. Woman is crucial to this harmonization. By fulfilling her 'natural' role as wife/mother she acts as a pivotal point around which the tensions in these dichotomies are resolved. They are resolved, however, at considerable cost to the woman who is neither citizen nor, strictly speaking, woman at all. Rather, she is reduced to the role of wife/mother. By privatizing familial concerns and making them the special province of women, Rousseau leaves men free to move between the private world – where 'natural' relations between the sexes and between fathers and children are conducted – and the public world of culture, citizenship and politico-ethical relations with other men. These two self-contained spheres allow him to split his own, possibly inconsistent, needs and desires into two domains. Since these are separated, they present little danger to his enjoyment of both.

The story of his wife, however, is quite different. She is not a citizen, she does not share the (theoretically) equitable relations of the free market, in fact she is not a political animal at all. She has been defined only in terms relative to men and male needs. In the case of Rousseau this is evident from the layout of *Emile*. Sophy makes her appearance in book 5, the last book, at that point where Emile needs to marry, to have children and to become a head of a household, which he must if he is to take up his rightful place in culture. What Sophy represents for Rousseau is the natural base and guarantee for the artificiality of culture. The significance of the claim that natural relations are timeless is clear. If relations between men and women do change, these changes are the result of artifice and corruption since natural relations are *by definition* static.

It was noted in chapter 2 that the seventeenth-century philosophers, Hobbes and Locke, both argue that men and women were equal in the state of nature. In the *Discourse*[22] Rousseau also allows that women in the state of nature possess equal capacity with men in fending for themselves. Why then do these philosophers consistently claim that women are naturally inferior in culture? An adequate response to this question requires the consideration of another philosophical construction, the social contract. Whatever disagreements philosophers have concerning the form and the legitimacy of the social contract, they universally agree that it is a contract entered into by men only. The significance of this is that women are, conceptually at least, still in a state of nature. Even contemporary theorists, such as Rawls, make this assumption. Women, therefore, lack a political existence and the benefits of such an existence, such as the protection of the state. This makes women vulnerable to the 'whims' of men, who are not bound by the usual laws of the body politic in their treatment of women. Ironically this arrangement also presents a threat to the state since women are internal to its operations yet not bound, by contract, to its rules and ideals. Hence, it is common, in the eighteenth century, to find women being conceptualized as uncivilized and hostile to reason and law. Rousseau remarked on the 'disorder' of women[23] and Hume on their propensity to the violent and socially disruptive passions.[24] The coercion required to ensure that women do not disrupt the political body created by men is not seen as political since men's relation to women is regarded as having its basis in *natural* rather than *political* authority.

The difficulty involved in trying to demonstrate, in terms consistent with eighteenth-century political discourses, that the relation of men to women is one of political dominance, is evidence of the power of the dichotomies which dominate those discourses. Man's relation to woman is familial and families are not appropriate objects of study for political philosophy. What is appropriate to political philosophy is the relationship of the family, as a structure, to the state. Or, put another way, the relationship between a man as head of a household and the state. This philosophical construction of nature and the associations between nature, women and the family, is important to address for at least two reasons. First, the particular construction of nature in the eighteenth century was an important underpinning to the viability of the social contract and women's exclusion from it. The construction of private, familial interests as natural, and political and economic interests as cultural allows the identity of man to be split into a private paternal authority and a fraternally constituted public citizen. These identities are both spatially and conceptually separated. Second, this construction of nature allows the depiction of women as the enemies of civilization – which, of course, means *patriarchal* civilization. The response of Rousseau to this situation is typical. He recommends the segregation of female and male concerns and asserts that the masculine public sphere should be invested with the ultimate authority in cases of conflict. In other words, it is masculine interests which take precedence over both familial and feminine ones.

The particular manner in which woman is constructed as the guardian of familial interests, and the opposing of these interests to the public sphere, actually predisposes women to be the enemies of public life. The theoretical justifications for women's exclusion from the public sphere and the consequent collapsing of familial and female interests are circular or self-fulfilling. Woman is constructed as close to nature, subject to passion and disorder, and so excluded from the rational body politic, which then constructs her as its internal enemy, or as Hegel phrases it, as its 'everlasting irony'.[25] Feminist theorists, at least from Wollstonecraft, have tried to point out that much of the irony involved in the contradictions between women's public and private existence stems from the contradictory demands put upon them by the masculine body politic. A discursive analysis of how political philosophy constructs its objects of study goes some way toward grasping how these paradoxes and ironies of female existence are created. It also shows why, when a political theory is treated as sex-neutral, women will figure, in those theories, as deficient. In this way this approach to various philosophical theories reverses the tendency of philosophy to pose women as the problem.

This third approach, which has here been called the feminist critique of philosophy, inverts the traditional understanding of the relation between human nature and culture. One such traditional understanding can be found in *The Principles of Philosophy* where Descartes describes philosophy as being like a tree: metaphysics being the roots that are not visible but essential; physics being the trunk and the branches being all the other aspects of philosophy, including ethics and politics.[26] His point in using this metaphor is that the extremities of the tree, including its fruit, cannot be understood or improved without a thorough knowledge of the tree as a complete organic system. The ethico-political theory of Descartes is notoriously spare and, according to the philosopher himself, this is because ethics and politics are, necessarily, the last objects of knowledge to be reached by reason. Put another way, if we are to understand and improve human social and political existence then we must first understand the principles of human nature, initially as a particular and then in relation to the regulative system of nature as a whole. This is the way that Hobbes, Locke, Hume, Rousseau and Mill all proceed. The answer to the first query, 'what essentially is a human being?', sets determining limits to what kind of social, political and ethical organization is thought to be suitable to it.

In these theorists' work human nature is thought to have an essentially constant and universal character that is, in differing degrees, considered to be mutable: improvable or corruptible. The kind of social and political organization and the ethical and legal principles that are to govern that organization are deduced from what a human being is thought to be, what its needs, desires, capabilities and limitations are. Once this problem is fathomed, the management of groups of such beings is largely a matter of deduction from these first principles. What must be kept in mind here, however, is that this mode of philosophizing involves a *formal* conception of human nature or human essence.

The introduction of the notion of a socially constructed subject,[27] which is a notion absolutely central to feminist theory, undermines the coherence of much traditional political philosophy. The following chapter will highlight the importance of this notion. To view human being as a social product devoid of determining universal characteristics is to view its possibilities as open-ended. This is not to say that human being is not constrained by historical context or by rudimentary biological facts but rather that these factors set the outer parameters of possibility only. Within these constraints, if they can be called that, there is a variety of possibilities.

The third response of feminists to philosophy affirms the possibility of a productive relation between the two. This developing feminist philosophy involves neither the obsolescence of feminism or philosophy, but hopefully the transformation of both. The salient point to make here is that, *contra* Daly and Spender, there cannot be an unadulterated feminist theory which would announce our arrival at a place where we could say we are 'beyond' patriarchal theory and patriarchal experience. Nor, *contra* Richards, can there be a philosophy which would be neutral, universal or truly *human* in its character, thus rendering feminism redundant.

This developing perspective, informed by both feminist theory and philosophy, offers the means of beginning to conceptualize and live – in an intertwined way – other forms of political and ethical being. In particular, a feminist philosophy can offer an integrated, though not closed, conception of being that acknowledges the connections between being and knowing, between politics and ethics, and between bodies and minds. This project, for feminists, has an urgency that prohibits its depiction as an ideal or merely abstract theoretical exercise. Compliantly living the social significance of the female body is no longer even a *practical* possibility for many women. This point was made in connection with my criticisms of McMillan. The traditional ideals of womanhood and femininity conflict with the lived reality of women today.

Some feminists are engaged in the deconstruction of these traditional ideals and the construction of other meanings and other significances of female experience.[28] The further erosion of dominant modes of interpretation of life and values is necessary. It has been argued here that the disjunctive relations internal to the reason/passion, mind/body and nature/culture dichotomies must be eroded. Feminist utilizations of psychoanalytic theory and deconstruction have opened one path which offers a means of conceptualizing reason and emotion, the mind and the body, nature and culture, without assuming a dichotomous structuring to these distinctions.

6

Psychoanalysis and French Feminisms

In the 1970s, psychoanalysis had a marked impact on socio-political theory, including feminist theory. Social theorists saw in psychoanalysis, not simply a therapeutic practice for the mentally ill, but a body of theory that could be used to shed light on the origins and functioning of society. In short, psychoanalytic theory came to be employed as cultural anthropology. Of course, this was not a novel use of psychoanalysis. Freud, himself, had written several pieces which hypothesized the origins of social life, of morality and the means by which cultures reproduce themselves across time.[1]

Although Freud himself was not explicit about his metaphysical commitments, it is clear that they do not include a dualistic conceptualization of mind and body, reason and emotion or nature and culture. Moreover, much of his work may be read as self-conscious, if infrequently successful, attempts to escape from this conceptual heritage.[2]

An important aspect of psychoanalytic theory is that it does not assume the existence of an *a priori* 'self' or 'ego'.[3] Rather, personal identity is developed in specific social and historical contexts.

Another important aspect of psychoanalytic theory which makes it particularly attractive to some social theorists is that it does not suppose the existence of specific innate or *a priori* instincts. In fact, Freud usually avoided the term *Instinkt* [instinct], preferring instead the term *Trieb* [drive].[4] Unfortunately, the Standard Edition of Freud's works translates both *Trieb* and *Instinkt* as instinct. This is unfortunate because it obscures the insight that human beings do not experience 'instincts' in any straightforwardly biological way. According to Freud, an instinct cannot be an object of consciousness – only the idea that represents the instinct can. Even in the unconscious, moreover, an instinct cannot be represented otherwise than by an idea.[5]

Thus, the concept of 'drive' is 'one of those lying on the frontier between the mental and the physical'.[6] The importance of the distinction between drive and instinct is that it allows one to consider the way in which particular cultures convert so-called natural or innate instincts into socialized drives. Thus, the 'sexual instinct', which on Freud's view does not have a natural, or in any sense innate, object, becomes, through various socialization practices a sexual *drive* whose object is culturally and historically specific.

Psychoanalytic theory is important in the context of this book because it has provided feminists with a theoretical framework capable of articuting the *social* meaning and significance of biology. Rather than contesting the 'natural' role of women, psychoanalysis offers the means to challenge the very category of the 'natural' and focus instead on the way in which bodies, whatever their capacities, are socially produced as *sexed* bodies. This shifts the emphasis from nature and biology to the ways in which bodies are encoded and trained by social practices and institutions, such as the family, to *become* masculine or feminine subjects. If human culture bears only an indirect relation to so-called natural instincts and if human identity is socially constructed, it seems reasonable to assume that present social relations are mutable. Moreover, if one could understand the means whereby society reproduces itself from one generation to the next, the possibilities for altering the character of society seem open. It is with precisely these concerns that Juliet Mitchell turned to psychoanalysis, in her book *Psychoanalysis and Feminism*.[7]

Psychoanalysis and Feminism was first published in 1974. It is a text which exemplifies feminist attempts to *extend* existing social theories so that they may take account of women's specificity. Mitchell attempts to draw together insights from anthropology, Marxism and psychoanalysis. She understands herself to be offering a theory which combines various aspects of social life – the economic, the ideological, the political – into a coherent whole. Her main objection to the employment of existentialism by feminists is that it is an overly individualistic theory of human existence that does not pay enough attention to economic and ideological considerations. Mitchell is also very critical of the existentialist rejection of the unconscious and its effects on the way we live our lives as sexed male or female subjects.

1 The Unconscious and Ideology

The Freudian theory of the unconscious is indispensable to an adequate understanding of the character and functioning of patriarchal culture since, Mitchell claims, 'the patriarchal law speaks to and through each person in his unconscious.'[8] Marxism too, Mitchell sees as crucial to any adequate social theory: it is a necessary but not sufficient component of a feminist analysis of culture. What she attempts in *Psychoanalysis and Feminism* is a melding together of both Marxist and psychoanalytic theory, where Marxism is intended to explain those features of human society that relate to the production and reproduction of human life at a material or economic level and psychoanalysis is meant to explain those features of human society that relate to the production and reproduction of patriarchal ideology at the level of ideas or mental life. Importantly, this level includes *unconscious* mental life.

What is it about psychoanalysis that Mitchell finds so indispensable to a feminist social theory? She argues, in the introduction to *Psychoanalysis and Feminism*, that psychoanalysis should not be read as a *prescription* for, but rather as a *description* of, patriarchal society.[9] The vehement rejection of Freud and psychoanalysis by irate feminists is misplaced, since if we are to understand the cultural devaluation of women then we need some understanding of how that devaluation operates unconsciously. Freud's writings constitute not only an analysis of the workings of the abnormal or maladjusted mind but also of normality itself and the way in which that normality is socially constructed. Put another way, normality is not innate and abnormality an aberration of this innate disposition, rather, both are products of extremely complex and often *unconscious* social relations and cultural interdictions. Hence, Freud's account of the way in which biological entities become social subjects is one which goes deeper into the construction of social roles and norms than any other social theory. In particular, his account of the way in which human beings become masculine and feminine subjects is more profound than, for example, sex-role theory.[10]

Freud, perhaps with the exception of Rousseau, is a unique figure in the history of Western thought in that he pays so much attention to sexual difference: for him the human subject is always a *sexed* subject. For these reasons, Mitchell claims, he should be studied by feminists as a theorist who offers an account of how biological males and females become particular kinds of social subjects.

If read properly, Mitchell argues, psychoanalysis can be understood as a theory, not about biology and instincts, but about the social *significance* of that biology and of the way in which instincts are converted to *drives*.

Psychoanalysis does not deny that we are biological organisms or that we are driven by various instincts. Rather, it stresses that we live this biology and these instincts not in nature but in *culture*, and moreover that the effect of culture is to transform and channel biology and instinct in particular ways. Anatomy is not the question here. The question is rather 'what is the cultural and social significance of anatomy?' or, put differently, 'how is anatomy represented in culture?' As she writes in the introduction:

> psychoanalysis is about the material reality of ideas both within, and of, man's history; thus in 'penis-envy' we are talking not about an anatomical organ, but about the ideas of it that people hold and live by within the general culture, the order of human society.[11]

In other words, we are not so much concerned with the *truth* of human biology but rather with the social and cultural *meaning* or *significance* of biology.

Psychoanalysis can offer an account of how 'the human animal with a bisexual psychological disposition becomes the sexed social creature – the man or the woman'.[12] The two key elements of this account are: first, Freud's analysis of infantile sexuality and second, Freud's account of the unconscious, its workings and its effects in everyday life.

Mitchell argues that feminists ignore these discoveries at their peril. We have seen throughout the development of this study that various feminists have viewed the oppression of women as being due to various *external* causes, such as the legal system, education, economic factors, lack of adequate political participation, and so on. Mitchell argues that all these factors could be altered yet women's position would not change in so far as they would still be defined in relation to man-as-the-norm. As de Beauvoir had attempted to show, part of the problem of woman's situation is her status as Other – man's other. The psychoanalytic accounts of infantile sexuality and of the unconscious offer a theory of how woman comes to be defined in terms only relative to man.

Infantile sexuality

Freud argued that very little of what we call adult sexuality can be viewed as innate or natural. Theories that maintain that sexuality arises at puberty in response to physiological, chemical or hormonal influences are rejected by Freud. Adult sexuality is an end product, the result of a long developmental process, and is never completely detached from its infantile origins. Freud offers an account of the way in which, from birth, a child's sexuality is channelled in certain directions, repressed in others and constructed in still other ways. The primitive opposition is not male/female, or even masculine/feminine, but rather active/passive. It may be seen as the task of culture to ensure that male = masculine = active and female = feminine = passive. These equations are, however, culturally constructed, not innate.

Freud contends that all human beings are initially bisexual or *polymorphously perverse*. These 'perverse' aspects of our sexuality do not disappear, rather they are all, if normality is to achieved, subsumed under the reproductive function. Thus, an adult interest in kissing, looking, exhibiting and other forms of 'foreplay' is not perverse, provided that these activities eventually result in heterosexual intercourse. A person is labelled 'perverse' only if these polymorphous pleasures refuse to bow to the demands of reproduction.

Obviously, this theory of sexual identity has quite radical repercussions. There is no 'natural' sexuality on Freud's view; sexuality is not innate or simply biological. Many contingent events can steer it from the path of reproduction. It is true, however, that on his account the polymorphous sexuality of the pre-oedipal child must be repressed if we are to become social beings capable of sustaining culture. He argues that much of the energy necessary to sustain culture is itself derived from the sublimation of these primary impulses. In other words, civilization itself is only achieved, and sustained, at the cost of various repressions.[13]

Although these processes of repression and discipline occur throughout a child's early years, through the oral, anal and phallic phases, it is not until the age of four or five that the child, by way of the Oedipus complex, *internalizes* these restrictions and demands from culture. That is, the child himself or herself feels displeasure at failing to comply with various interdictions. Here the possibility of guilt and neurosis arise. It is important to stress the obvious: it is largely through the vehicle of sexuality that the child is socialized, that is, through sexual pleasure and the processes of sexual differentiation. This socialization acts directly on and through the body of the child and the pleasures of that body. Hence, personal identity is always, and fundamentally, an embodied, *sexed* identity. This internalization of social rules and prohibitions results, at least for boys, in what Freud calls the superego. The superego is the internalized rules and prohibitions of the parents and of the culture. It is only at this point that we could say we are now dealing with a *social* creature.

In the case of the boy the formation of the superego takes place by way of the castration complex. The young boy learns that his close association with his mother cannot continue indefinitely. The mother is the property of the father, who has greater phallic power than the boy. The child, according to Freud, interprets his father's power as a threat to his bodily integrity: that is, he fears the father will castrate him if he does not give up the desire for his mother. This fear is given force and credence, Freud argues, by the sight of female genitals. The male child does not see sexual *difference*, he sees *lack*.[14]

It is important to stress here that sexual difference, so poorly understood by very young children, is nevertheless a subject of great fascination for them. The lesser social power and apparent less social worth of women may be understood, from this immature perspective, as being a result of their castration: that is, these creatures, who seem to be of less value have been punished by the powerful father for past disobediences. In any case, it seems important to question *why* it is that children of both sexes, at least at a crucial age, see sexual difference in terms of (one) presence and (its) absence rather than in terms of (two) different presences.[15] The boy surmounts the Oedipus complex once he accepts his father's right to his mother which involves also accepting the father's authority, that is, patriarchal authority. The male child must, moreover, identify with this power since provided he has the phallus, he has access to patriarchal power and eventually to a woman/wife of his own. To refuse the father's power may result in the boy choosing homosexuality as a means of retaining both the phallus and his attachment to his mother.

The story of the little girl is quite different. Whereas with the boy the castration complex puts an end to the Oedipus complex – as Freud says it 'shatters' it[16] – the girl enters the castration complex *first* and it is a quite different kind of complex for her: specifically, castration is a *fait accompli*. This led Freud to abandon the symmetry he initially entertained between the two sexes, where the girl loves her father and takes her mother as her rival. Freud postulated, rather late in his career, the existence of the 'dark continent' of femininity. He also likened the dark and 'shadowy' pre-oedipal feminine phase to the 'Minoan-Mycenaean' culture which is overlaid by that of the (masculine) Greek.[17] The first love object for the girl is also the mother; her sexuality, according to Freud, is also phallic (clitoral). In fact, Freud says, 'we are obliged to call the little girl, a little *man*.'[18] For her the Oedipus complex is a secondary formation, and has much less psychical force than the castration complex. She turns to her father, her sex-appropriate love object, only by default. The realization of her own castration along with that of her mother and of all women, inflicts upon the girl a great psychical blow, from which, Freud says, she never fully recovers.[19] She has less motivation for leaving the Oedipus complex with the result that the formation of her superego suffers. This, in turn, results in her having a poor sense of justice and an antagonistic attitude toward civilization and its demands.[20]

Freud says there are three options open to the girl. First, she may turn away from sexuality altogether; this may result in sexual frigidity. Second, she may retain the 'masculine' activity which she had enjoyed up until the castration complex and refuse the 'fact' of castration. This option Freud calls the masculinity complex and the result may be homosexuality.

Finally, the girl may turn to the father, initially in the hope of getting a penis. When that wish has been transformed into a wish for a child from a father-substitute, normal femininity is attained. In Freud's terms: 'The girl has turned into a little woman.'[21]

Freud makes much of the fact that for the girl the processes of acculturation are comparatively arduous.[22] She must transfer her affections from the mother to the father; transfer her erotogenic zone from the clitoris to the vagina; and most importantly, surrender her pre-oedipal activity in favour of passivity and passive aims. The more fortunate boy retains his original love object (the mother, or, mother-substitutes), his original erotogenic zone and his activity. Feminine sexuality, on the contrary, is passive in its character: normal femininity can 'invite' but not initiate. This accession of the male and female to their respective masculine and feminine roles is succinctly summarized by Freud in the following terms:

> Maleness *combines* [the factors of] subject, activity and possession of the penis; femaleness *takes over* [those of] object and passivity. The vagina is now valued as a place of shelter for the penis; it enters into the heritage of the womb.[23]

There are several complex problems with Freud's account of femininity and womanhood. Here I will mention only two. First, as many feminists have argued, his view of infantile sexuality is *phallocentric*, that is, it recognizes only one organ: the penis/phallus.[24] Up until the Oedipus complex, Freud argues that children of both sexes assume a phallic world. The girl's sexuality is no less active or phallic than the boy's and both, being ignorant of the existence of the vagina, assume that the mother has a phallus. Several feminists have argued against this view, claiming that it denies, or more pertinently *disavows*, the specificity of feminine eroticism.[25] The second problem with Freud's account of femininity is captured by his infamous phrase: 'anatomy is destiny.'[26] The feminist objection to this claim has its basis in Freud's own work. It is not *anatomy* that decides cultural value or status but rather the way in which that anatomy is represented and lived. As shall be shown below, it is this notion of the psychical representation of anatomy – or *morphology* – that French feminists use in order to argue for a notion of femininity that is not simply the inverse, or the negative, of masculinity.

The unconscious

The Oedipus complex serves at least two important functions. First, it creates *appropriate* human subjects for the particular culture in which it occurs. In that the basic structure of the complex involves the child, the object of desire and the law which bars the child's access to the object of desire, socialized desire is always desire that has been modified by the law. Second, it *sexes* subjects. Post-oedipal subjects are, ideally, *either* masculine males or feminine females. Inappropriate patterns, impulses or desires are repressed. For example, the boy's previous passivity and the girl's previous activity should be repressed. They become part of the contents of the unconscious, as does the Oedipus complex itself. In this way one could understand the unconscious as the repository of all that culture wishes to keep at a distance, to forbid or to censor.

We know of the existence of the unconscious, according to Freud, by way of jokes, dreams and parapraxes. These three features of mental life act as compromises, of a sort, between unconscious desires and the demands of consciousness (the ego and the superego).[27] They act as compromises by disguising the unconscious wish, desire or demand. This is taken to be a startling discovery because we can no longer assume that mental life is equivalent to consciousness. Consciousness is merely the visible tip of the iceberg.

We can begin to see why, for Mitchell, psychoanalysis is so important. For, if women's social status is connected not only to consciousness, to material and economic factors, but also to the unconscious, then no amount of social change or consciousness-raising will alter the unconscious determinants of cultural attitudes toward women. What we need, on her view, is an account which would show the way in which ideology operates unconsciously. She writes:

> The concept of the unconscious is a concept of mankind's transmission and inheritance of his social (cultural) laws. In each man's unconscious lies all mankind's 'ideas' of his history; a history that cannot start afresh with each individual but must be acquired and contributed to over time. Understanding the laws of the unconscious thus amounts to a start in understanding how ideology functions, how we acquire and live the ideas and laws within which we must exist.[28]

Mitchell's account of the unconscious and ideology relies on the work of French Marxist, Louis Althusser. In 'Ideology and Ideological State Apparatuses' he distinguishes two forms of state power: repressive state apparatuses, which include coercive forms of state power such as the police force and the army, and ideological state apparatuses, which include schools, religion and the family.[29] Althusser attempted to draw a distinction between science and ideology where aspects of Marxist and psychoanalytic theory could together offer a scientific account of the material and psychic conditions of life. He used Jacques Lacan's structuralist reading of Freud to argue that the unconscious is the domain of the production and reproduction of ideology. I will have more to say about Lacan later in this chapter.

At this point it is important to signal that Mitchell employs a structuralist model in her reading of Freud. On this model masculine and feminine subjects are the product of a complex set of structures (economic, familial, religious) within which each must 'recognize' him-or herself as, for example, white, working class, woman. Such recognition is the effect of social practices and structures not, as common sense may imply, simply a recognition of one's 'nature'. The fact that subjects apparently 'naturally' recognize themselves and each other as masculine or feminine, white or black, working class or middle class, is itself an effect of ideology. Put differently, on Althusser's view ideology has the structure of both recognition and misrecognition. Human subjects recognize themselves and each other as particular kinds of social subjects but they misrecognize the origin of their particularity as given by nature. There are problems with this account which will be raised shortly.[30]

Whilst *Psychoanalysis and Feminism* presents arguments for the indispensability of psychoanalytic theory to feminist theory, it merely assumes the indispensability of Marxism. What Mitchell envisaged was the dual application of Marxism and psychoanalysis to the relatively autonomous spheres of capitalism and class, on the one hand, and patriarchy and sex, on the other. Again, Mitchell assumes rather than argues for the autonomy of capitalism and patriarchy. She understands patriarchy as the 'rule of the father' and positions it in a kinship system which she argues is more suitable to a feudal than a capitalist society. It is this assumption of the *archaic* nature of patriarchy as linked to kinship systems, exogamy and the exchange of women, that allows her to posit capitalist society as posing inevitable contradictions to the situation of women and the family: contradictions, she argues, that can and should be aggravated by feminist political struggle. As she sees it, the nuclear family is the site of the contradictions between patriarchy and capitalism since the 'supposedly natural nuclear family would be in harsh contradiction to the kinship structure as it is articulated in the Oedipus complex.'[31] Hence, the necessity to struggle against both capitalism and patriarchy, maximizing those points of tension *between* the two systems.

Mitchell is claiming that capitalism presents a challenge to patriarchy since it is a form of social organization that does not endorse the rule of the father; nor does it require the taboo on incest nor the exchange of women. However, Mitchell's understanding of patriarchy is open to question. The definition of patriarchy as the 'rule of the father' has been challenged in recent times by many feminists. For example, Carole Pateman in 'The Fraternal Social Contract', argues that modern patriarchy should be understood as *fraternal* rather than paternal, and as based on civil and contractual rather than kinship relations. In short, patriarchy is not an archaic system that is redundant or irrelevant to present social relations. On the contrary, patriarchy in its modern fraternal form underpins the social contract which is the foundation for modern civil society.[32]

Another weakness in Mitchell's presentation of psychoanalysis and its utility to feminism is her cursory treatment of the unconscious. Most of her comments on the unconscious involve placing it as the site of ideology. Given that the unconscious contains nothing but *representations*, it is necessary to offer some analysis of the relation between language and the unconscious. Mitchell does not do this.[33] The problem is most glaring in her (partial) importation of Jacques Lacan's reading of Freud.[34] Lacan incorporated insights from Claude Lévi-Strauss's structural anthropology and Ferdinand de Saussure's structuralist theory of language into his reading of Freud. Saussure argued that linguistic elements do not signify in isolation or by virtue of any relation of correspondence to their 'objects'. Rather, language is a system of interrelated elements which signify by virtue of their *difference* from one another. Meaning, then, is generated by the relations among or between the elements of language. Lévi-Strauss posited that every society is governed by a series of interrelated structures (of kinship, ritual and myth) and that in order to understand how human subjects and cultural beliefs are produced within any given culture, one needs to be able to recognize and analyse these structures.

Lacan uses the work of both Saussure and Lévi-Strauss in his analysis of the unconscious, claiming that it is governed by structures like those which govern language. The primary psychical processes identified by Freud – condensation and displacement – operate, according to Lacan, analogously to the way metaphor and metonymy do in language. Just as human subjects, in order that they *become* subjects, must become speaking subjects in a language which exists before them, so too must they enter the pre-existing structures of the Symbolic order of culture via the Oedipus complex. This is what it is to become a human subject in culture. Of course, subjects in culture are not aware of the structures which determine their place and value in society. Rather they live within these structures much as one can live in language without being aware of its formative effects.

Whereas common sense would suggest that I speak language, structuralist theory would insist that language speaks me. Lacanian psychoanalysis attempts to account for how unconscious structures speak subjects, construct their desires and give rise to their neuroses. It is beyond the scope of this work to enter into the details of this tradition in any depth and several excellent accounts of Lacan, structuralism and their relation to feminism are available.[35] However, it is important to note here that Mitchell's use of Lacan, in the context of psychoanalytic feminism, raises problems. On the one hand, Mitchell accepts the structuralist account of the creation of subjects in culture, but on the other hand she appears to want to maintain the intelligibility of voluntarist political action. It is not clear how this can be done. If the human subject is an effect of its structural position, on what basis does political action rest? It is at this point that Mitchell's attempt to synthesize structuralism, Marxism, feminism and psychoanalysis is most strained. Her implicit appeal to Althusser's distinction between science and ideology only compounds the problem. On Althusser's account, psychic life itself seems to be reduced to the ideological. What remains as 'science' are those elements of Marxist and psychoanalytic theory that the structuralist perspective has managed to recoup. But the scientific status of structuralist theory is undermined by its own claim that meaning is always relational. This relational and contextual generation of meaning renders absolute knowledge claims problematic. What is the relation between a theory and the culture it purports to understand? Under which conditions can a theory be counted as a true theory? Structuralism poses structures as the origin of meaning but knowledge of these structures is assumed to be independent of the social conditions under which such knowledge is produced.

It is partly in response to these sorts of problems that post-structuralists, such as Michel Foucault, embarked upon a Nietzschean analysis of the conditions under which knowledge and truth are produced. Taking the structuralist position to its breaking point, Foucault claims that truth itself is an effect of discourses. This claim undermines the basis on which the science/ideology distinction rests. Ideology, according to Foucault,

> always stands in virtual opposition to something else which is supposed to count as truth. Now, I believe that the problem does not consist in drawing the line between that in a discourse which falls under the category of scientificity or truth, and that which comes under some other category, but in seeing historically how effects of truth are produced in discourses which in themselves are neither true nor false.[36]

It is unclear, from the post-structuralist perspective, why *a priori* status should be granted to structures, since they derive their meaning by standing in some relation to other elements in discourse. The epistemological privilege accorded to structures does not stand up under close scrutiny. In the context of Mitchell's attempt to understand the unconscious as the site of the production and reproduction of ideology, the epistemological privilege appears to lie with material economic and political structures, with psychic life and sexual difference being understood as superstructural effects. In this sense, Mitchell's use of psychoanalysis served to incorporate women into Marxist theory without posing a threat to the priority of the economic category of class.

As will be shown, in the next section, Luce Irigaray and Hélène Cixous are less accepting than Mitchell of some of the fundamental assumptions of structuralism and Lacanian psychoanalysis.

2 Ecriture Féminine and the Return of the Repressed

In chapter 5 of *Sexual/Textual Politics*, Toril Moi observes that:

> Whereas the American feminists of the 1960s had started by vigorously denouncing Freud, the French took it for granted that psychoanalysis could provide an emancipatory theory of the personal and a path to the exploration of the unconscious, both of vital importance to the analysis of the oppression of women in patriarchal society.[37]

Moi has pointed to an important difference between Anglo-American feminisms and French feminisms, but more needs to said for the point to make its impact. Here I will make two points that I take to be crucial.

The first point is that Anglo-American feminisms, whilst rejecting Freud, wholeheartedly embraced what may be called 'anti-psychiatry' and 'liberation' theories: for example, the writings of R. D. Laing, David Cooper, Paolo Freire and Franz Fanon. What these theorists share, diverse though they are, is the idea that verbalizing, speaking and literacy are in themselves liberating activities. The implicit notion is that part of what is involved in oppression is the unreflective living of one's social reality. The first step toward liberation was understood to be the conscious exploration of the ideological conditions of social life.

A typical case of this kind of politics can be recognized in the practice of consciousness-raising: a group of women come to realize that their particular dissatisfactions and apparent failings are widely shared by others. Hence the problem is not simply an individual, but a social, one. It is not you or I who are maladjusted, but the system itself that is oppressive. It is the public verbalization of oppression and the sharing of common oppressive experiences that was, in itself, seen as liberating. This view assumes that there is an essential 'I' or 'self' that needs to be freed from oppressive social relations. It assumes that it is possible to get beyond 'ideology' to the 'true' nature of our existence and our social relations. The philosophical orientation of this theory is, then, profoundly *humanist*. Underneath ideology and social oppression, lies the 'true' or essential person. The work of Mary Daly, which was considered in chapter 4, is clearly influenced by this kind of humanism.

The second point which needs to be raised, if Moi's remarks are to carry the force that they should, is that French feminists did not embrace just any old Freud (there are several); they embraced Lacan's Freud.[38] French feminists, unlike their Anglo-American counterparts, are much more closely aligned with philosophical than sociological theories. And Lacan's version of Freud is a highly philosophical one. It may well be this philosophical underpinning to much French feminism that makes it relatively inaccessible to many Anglo-American readers.

Elaine Marks stresses four distinct influences on French feminists: linguistic and structuralist theory (Saussure and Lévi-Strauss); Marxism (particularly Althusser); psychoanalytic theory (particularly Lacan); and deconstruction (Derrida).[39] Some mention has been made above, of Saussure, Lévi-Strauss, Lacan and Althusser. It remains to offer some account of Derrida and the relation between deconstruction and contemporary feminism. Derrida's project involves the radical questioning of the binary oppositions (culture/nature, self/other, presence/absence, man/woman) foundational to Western metaphysics. Derrida maintains, along with structuralists, that these oppositions derive their meaning from the dynamic interrelation between terms: culture can be defined only by reference to nature, man derives his identity from defining himself against woman, and so on. Yet, he criticizes structuralist theory for preserving a hierarchy within these oppositions by positing one of the terms as primary. He points out that both psychoanalysis and philosophy privilege presence over absence, identity over difference and man over woman.[40] Derrida's strategy is to demonstrate that such privilege is unfounded since identity, presence and the unitary self are not only elusive but illusory. Virginia Hules explains that on Derrida's view

[the] present exists only by virtue of its relationship to the past and the future. Thus, the present is an impossible composite – no superposition uniting the three can ever occur. The relation of present self to past meaning, as that of the present to itself, is one of irremediable 'differance', a term by which Derrida designates not only the notion of the inherent multiplicity underlying all 'unity', but also temporal displacement, a continual deferring of unity implying that absence is an intrinsic property of presence.[41]

Derrida demonstrates the conditionality of identity, presence and man by finding *within* each term that which it seeks to define itself against. This move has obvious implications for feminist politics. If 'woman' has meaning only in relation to its opposite 'man', and if 'man' is implicated in what it means to be a 'woman', then a politics which bases itself on the irreducibility and specificity of women's experience is bound to result in contradiction and incoherence. Deconstruction aims to show that the other is always implied in any definition of the self, that is, the self is not identical with itself. Feminists must either respond that 'woman' bears no relation to women or their experiences – an unconvincing claim in the context of the history of philosophy, as I have endeavoured to show in earlier chapters of this book – or accept the fragmentation of past universalizing claims of feminist politics concerning 'woman'.

The three terms which, in chapter 3, I took to be crucial to de Beauvoir's study of woman – 'female', 'the feminine', 'woman' – reappear here in a different guise. De Beauvoir maintained that feminine traits and those aspects of the female body that were seen as debilitating should be transcended in order that woman could emerge unshackled. Only by taking the female body and femininity as *her* other could woman hope to escape from the position of permanent other. From a deconstructive perspective this strategy is foredoomed since the masculinity which de Beauvoir treats as being of positive value would be contentless without femininity. Under the influence of deconstruction, both Irigaray and Cixous reverse de Beauvoir's strategy by re-instating the female body and the feminine and treating both as sites for exploration in feminist politics. Otherness, or alterity, is here linked positively to the issue of sexual difference. However, the aim is not the simple reversal of the hierarchy between man and woman, masculine and feminine, as I have claimed Daly's work does, but rather involves challenging and unsettling the coherence of the opposition itself. This aim is achieved by showing the ways in which woman, the feminine and female sexuality *exceed* the complementary role they have been assigned in the oppositions man/woman, masculine/feminine, phallic sexuality/castrated sexuality.

On this view, one of the most important struggles is to engage in the subversion of phallocentric discourses and to foster a language that is able to express the specificity of the feminine. On their view, *women* are not simply the *oppressed* in educational, legal or economic terms, but also the *feminine* is the *repressed*. The feminine is the repressed in language, in philosophy and in culture. As language is the only means of access to the unconscious, to that which is repressed, they stress the necessity for women to write/speak; not to write or speak *about* women, or their situation, but *as* women. Women must 'write their bodies', which amounts to 'writing the repressed'.[42] Repression involves denying that which is to be repressed access to consciousness, which is in turn achieved by denying it access to the pre-conscious and language.[43] If the condition of patriarchal society is the repression of the feminine, then that which writes/speaks of the feminine imaginary amounts to the return of the repressed. Writing of a full feminine form and of feminine desire involves the return to patriarchal consciousness of that which it has repressed. If we compare the aims of these writers with the aims of many Anglo-American writers, who seek a 'non-sexist' style of writing, we can begin to see the enormous gulf which separates these two theoretical approaches.

One begins to grasp that the very terms of the early Anglo-American programme for liberation are themselves antithetical to the basic tenets of French feminisms. In particular, French feminists might ask, 'how can a language, a literacy or a verbalization that is phallocentric be liberating for women?' In fact, it is the very terms of liberation theory that these theorists seek to subvert. The stress on humanism, on the coherent subject who can liberate her 'I', is precisely that element in the history of philosophy that these feminists seek to question, since it is *this* subject who has as *his* condition of possibility, the repression of difference and the repression of the feminine. Full, unalienated speech, in the sense understood by liberation theorists, is understood on this model as little more than the ability to speak, or write, *like a man*, as if I (a woman) were a man. This would amount to little more than alienating oneself in language 'as a man does', that is, it would be no liberation at all. All this would achieve is the strengthening of phallocentric discourses, in a manner analogous to the way in which, as was argued in chapter 2, women's admission to liberal society, on the *same* terms as men, merely strengthens the masculine privilege that is implicit in liberal society. The point is rather to reveal the conditions for the functioning of phallocentrism: specifically the repression of difference and of femininity. This aim would be one way of understanding what is meant by the phrase *'écriture féminine'*.

In what follows I will briefly consider the work of both Luce Irigaray and Hélène Cixous. I disagree with Moi's rendering of Cixous's work as concerned with a 'romanticized version of the *female body* as the site of women's writing'.[44] This view is based on a misunderstanding of the way in which both Irigaray and Cixous understand the body and sexual difference. This misunderstanding centres on the difference, mentioned above, between anatomy and morphology. The source of the problem is clear enough in Moi's own text, though she fails to recognize it. In talking about problems which arise for the English-speaking reader of French feminisms, she observes:

> In French there is only one adjective to 'femme', and that is 'féminin', whereas English has two adjectives to 'woman': 'female' and 'feminine'. It has long been recognized usage among many English-speaking feminists to use 'feminine' (and 'masculine') to represent social constructs (gender) and to reserve 'female' (and 'male') for purely biological aspects (sex). *The problem is that this fundamental political distinction is lost in French*. Does *écriture féminine*, for instance, mean 'female' or 'feminine' writing? How can we know whether this or any other such expression refers to sex or to gender?[45]

However, this objection misses the rather obvious point that sex and gender are *theoretical* constructs, not transcendent categories and the distinction is not so much *lost* in the French, as simply never made. The objection assumes that sex, a 'purely biological aspect' of sexual difference, can be represented transparently or 'neutrally', implying that sex has to do with facts (science) and gender has to do with values (ideology). In fact, in the last decade or so Anglo-American feminists have turned a very critical eye to the sex/gender distinction and its obvious complicity in mind/body dualism.[46] The absence of such a distinction in French may actually be seen as a strength of French feminist theory. Faced with the choice between understanding *écriture féminine* as 'feminine' writing or as 'female' writing, Moi opts for the latter course. Cixous's writing, Moi claims, is about the *female* body. This is to apply categories to Cixous's writing that are inappropriate. As Moi herself points out, in the above quotation, the distinction between the *female* body (anatomy), and the *feminine* body (social) is peculiar to the English language. This is certainly not to say that French feminists do not make a distinction between biological and social aspects of sexual difference. However, the distinction is not made in terms of another binary polarity, like sex and gender, but rather in terms of a middle term, a term that is *reducible* to neither anatomy nor socialization: that term is *morphology*.

When both Irigaray and Cixous speak of woman's body they speak in terms of its morphology, meaning the way in which the shape or form of the female body is represented in culture. Morphology is not given, it is interpretation, which is not to say that it has nothing to do with our cultural understandings of biology. Freud's morphological description of the female sex as castrated, as lacking, receives no more nor less 'confirmation' from biology than does Irigaray's positing of the female sex as made up of (at least) two lips.[47] The difference is that Freud's morphological description of the female sex amounts to the inverse of male morphology which is taken to be full, phallic; whilst Irigaray's description presents the female form as full, as lacking nothing. Both descriptions are clearly 'biased' or political but French feminists would deny that any discourse can be neutral or free from political investments.

What is interesting about the positing of a full female morphology is that it presents a challenge to the Freudian construction of sexual difference in terms of presence and absence (of the phallus). This construction represses or disavows *positive* difference, since it can conceive difference only on the model of *one* presence and its lack: that is, *no* difference. Of course, the feminist description of the female sex is no more, or less, *true* than is Freud's. Irigaray is quite clear on this, claiming that,

> the issue is not one of elaborating a new theory of which woman would be the *subject* or the *object*, but of jamming the theoretical machinery itself, of suspending its pretension to the production of a truth and of a meaning that are excessively univocal. Which presupposes that women do not aspire simply to be men's equals in knowledge . . . They [women] should not put it, then, in the form 'What is woman?' but rather, repeating/interpreting the

way in which, within discourse, the feminine finds itself defined as lack, deficiency, or as imitation and negative image of the subject, they should signify that with respect to this logic a *disruptive excess* is possible on the feminine side.[48]

Not a truth then, but an utterance of excess, that problematizes the truth and the way in which 'true' utterances are constituted. It is in this sense that Irigaray's claims concerning the isomorphic relation between the male form and Western discourse should be understood. The claim is not, necessarily, an essentialist or biologistic one where a causal relation is posited between male biology and male-produced discourse. Rather, the claim is that both Western discourse and the phallocentric construction of the male body are complicit each with the other. In 'Women's Exile' she puts it this way:

> The question of language is closely allied to that of feminine sexuality. For I do not think that language is universal or neutral with regard to the difference between the sexes. In the face of a language, constructed and maintained by men only, I raise the question of the specificity of a feminine language: of a language that would be adequate for the body, sex, and the imaginary of the woman. A language which presents itself as universal and which is in fact produced by men only, is this not what maintains the alienation and exploitation of women in and by society?[49]

Her aim, then, is not to join the academy and continue the production of its discourses, nor to make these discourses 'speak' the 'truth' of women, which one could see as the aim of other feminist projects, for example, those of Wollstonecraft and de Beauvoir. Rather, she attempts to 'speak' the specificity of herself as a woman, as the feminine, and in so doing to return to philosophy, or psychoanalysis, its own repressed. Speaking and writing from a position which acknowledges itself as feminine and corporeal makes visible the masculine perspective from which philosophy has been constructed. Giving voice to that which has been repressed in Plato's or Freud's text forces them to abandon their masks of neutrality and reveal that they too have a body, a sex and a perspective. Two present sexes – rather than one sex (the male) and its absence (the female) – introduces the possibility of genuine intercourse. Without two presences intercourse between the sexes could only result in rape. This has, too frequently, been the outcome of the writings of Plato and Freud: phallic entries on a mute feminine body.

For both Irigaray and Cixous the mutism of women is a fundamental feature of Western cultures. Women are forbidden speech, particularly in the public sphere.[50] Women are the assumed infrastructure of culture but cultural production requires only the acquiescence of their corporeality. Women are required to make their bodies available for exchange between men and for reproduction. Lévi-Strauss claimed that culture is based on the exchange of women, the exchange of women between *men*. Irigaray asks, 'but what if the commodities began to speak?'[51] How could they speak and still serve the function of the essential and commodified infrastructure of social life? Women's commodity status bars their access to social agency, including speech. They are not active social participants but the objects which circulate between social agents. In *The Sexual Contract*, Carole Pateman argues that social contract theorists assume that the (male) parties to the contract have sexual access to women. Citizens of the fraternity, she argues, are assumed to be husbands and (at least potential) fathers. Underlying the fraternal social contract, hidden and repressed, is a sexual contract. The fraternity of liberty and equality between men assumes a prior relation of domination and subordination between men and women.

Whether we look to political theory, anthropology or psychoanalysis for an account of women's social being, a consistent story emerges: women appear as the essential component that allows exchanges between men to take place. Lacan's formulation of the Symbolic realm of language and culture is not excepted, as will be shown shortly.[52] Women do not enter the Symbolic realm of language and culture as subjects capable of speaking their desire. Rather, women become the objects of a (foredoomed) masculine desire. Women do not become social agents but function as the 'natural' foundation for social relations. They are reduced to the level of mere corporeality, mere matter, out of which men fashion culture. I will return to this issue in chapter 7.

In 'Women's Exile', Irigaray claims that women are 'the depositories of the body', but this can only continue on the condition that women comply with 'normal femininity'. Such compliance amounts to women allowing themselves to be reduced to the role of wife/mother. For women to refuse to play this part would mean the end of their exploitation as the foundation for culture, its laws and its exchange system, while remaining excluded from it. This is what Irigaray attempts to do in relation to Western discourse: to disrupt its assumptions, to refuse to be mere body, to remind man that he too has a body. Perhaps then we could conceive of a mother who is still a woman. In this way, she offers another perspective from which to 'think' feminine specificity. The style of her language is deliberately ambiguous, paradoxical, poetic and metaphoric. This style mirrors the picture of feminine specificity that she presents, at the same time as it undermines the dominance of the phallic, the well-formed, clarity, singularity of meaning – in short, it refuses the values of mainstream philosophy.

Clearly then, I disagree with Moi's reading of *écriture féminine* as being concerned with woman's essence or biology. One of the most important insights of structuralism and psychoanalysis is precisely that we have no unmediated access to the 'real' body, the 'raw' or the 'natural' body. On the contrary, the human body and sexual difference are always *lived in culture*, mediated by its values, its oppositions and its discourses. Freud made a similar point when he claimed that we do not simply 'live' our instincts but rather the psychical *representation* of an instinct. The point made by Irigaray and Cixous is that the dominant representations of cultural life are masculine representations.

This point should not be confused with that made by Spender (see chapter 4 above). There is a crucial difference. Whereas Spender assumes that conscious male intentions encode patriarchal values into language, Irigaray and Cixous would shift the focus from maleness to masculinity, and from the conscious intentions of men to the unconscious determinants of patriarchal culture. Of course, it could be argued that this merely shifts the problem treated in Spender's work from the 'conscious intentions of men' to 'the unconscious determinants of culture'. In other words, it could be argued that both Irigaray and Cixous are caught in a similar paradox to Spender. After all, they maintain that women are condemned to mutism, on the one hand, and exhort women to write/speak as women, on the other. However, this objection would need to take account of the problematic existence of the unconscious. It is always possible that that which is repressed will return to consciousness. To make this point adequately it will be necessary to mention the work of Lacan and the challenge which Irigaray and Cixous present to his formulation of cultural life.

In the structuralist version of psychoanalysis, what has been called 'Lacan's Freud' (above, p. 112), neither the subject nor social life are posited as completed realities but rather as *processes*. Catherine Belsey puts it this way:

> the subject is . . . the site of contradiction, and is consequently perpetually
> in the process of construction, thrown into crisis by alterations in language
> and in the social formation, capable of change. And, in the fact that the
> subject is a *process* lies the possibility of transformation.[53]

Part of what is involved in the contradictory nature of human subjectivity, according to the Lacanian model, is that the subject is the site of repressions and prohibitions, specifically the repression of the imaginary. For both Irigaray and Cixous the imaginary, which roughly corresponds with the pre-oedipal period in Freud, is the source of feminine specificity. The phase itself may be understood as specifically feminine, regardless of the sex of the subject. To borrow Freud's analogy, it is the Minoan-Mycenaean culture, which lies hidden beneath the Greek.

The intervention of the Symbolic and the Law of the Father – roughly the oedipal period – transforms the primitive ego (moi), or the pre-oedipal subject, into a speaking subject, an 'I'.[54] But the subject emerges from this phase, what Lacan calls the breaking up of the dyadic mirror phase,[55] as a *sexed* subject, that is, as phallic or as castrated. In a sense we could say that this is the fully-fledged *patriarchal* subject. But prior to this stage the phallic/castrated opposition is absent. The imaginary is not destroyed or obliterated, it is *repressed*, and as such it remains part of the subject and of the social formation. It is revealed in dreams, in metaphor, in symptoms, in parapraxes and, of course in *literature*, particularly in certain kinds of *avant garde* writing. It is this repressed imaginary that I take French feminists to be referring to when they speak of the feminine imaginary, of feminine morphology and of *écriture féminine*.

Lacan argues that the imaginary must be repressed if *man* is to take up his position in culture as a speaking subject capable of entering relations of exchange. Irigaray points out that no such option exists for *woman*. Her place in (that) culture is to be an *object* of exchange and to be alienated from herself and her body in phallocentric language. For this reason she draws attention to the psychoanalytic assumption that the unconscious and language are sexually indifferent. Irigaray suggests that

> we might wonder whether certain properties attributed to the unconscious may not, in part, be ascribed to the female sex, which is censured by the logic of consciousness. Whether the feminine *has* an unconscious or whether it *is* the unconscious.[56]

In the aptly titled paper 'Castration or Decapitation?'[57] (even more apt in French: 'Le Sexe ou la tête?'), Cixous argues that women do not enter the Symbolic as speaking subjects, or at least, their speech cannot 'speak' their desire since they must occupy the position of the *object* of desire. *Active* feminine desire must be repressed and so remain unrepresented in the phallic economy. In that paper she argues that the phallic or masculine economy is dominated by the equation castration/debt/death. The masculine economy is always associated, unconsciously, with debt: debt to the father, debt to the Symbolic. It is debt incurred via the castration complex and being 'spared' the fate of becoming a woman. It is an economy where sexual *difference* is represented as sexual *opposition*, and oppositions, she says, always result in the death or repression of one of the terms. Here she is offering an implicit criticism of Hegel and his assumption that difference results in a conflictual opposition. De Beauvoir, as was shown in chapter 3, imports Hegel's view of difference into her consideration of sexual difference, claiming that 'the duality of the sexes, like any duality, gives rise to conflict.'[58] Cixous, on the contrary, wants to argue that the genuine acknowledgement of difference would not result in opposition but would allow a movement from one to the other and back again without conflict or death. This, she argues, is an economy where 'the gift' can function without incurring debt, that is, it is an economy outside the economy of castration/debt/death.

The masculine economy equates desire and death because masculine desire for the other (woman) inevitably brings itself 'face-to-face' with castration/death. This economy excludes the possibility of representing the feminine as anything other than castrated. Or, what amounts to the same thing, it only admits the feminine as decapitated. Since feminine castration is a *fait accompli*, there is no possibility of woman entering this system of exchange as a participant. She cannot be expected to obey its laws or to respect its 'currency'. Thus, woman must pay with her 'head', that is, her voice – she is reduced to silence, mutism or hysteria. Locked in the body, the body is all women have to express their madness. Hence, the prevalence of female hysterics in the nineteenth century and of female anorexics/bulimics in the twentieth.

The interaction of French feminisms with traditional or existing theories reveals its share of borrowing (from Lacan, from Derrida) yet it also reveals a critical depth. In particular, it argues for the possibility of creating a speaking position for female subjectivity, rather than simply adopting the authority of the theories they employ. Irigaray, for example, is clearly indebted to psychoanalytic and philosophical theory, yet her work is not simply an attempt to extend these theories to include women. Rather, her work is an attempt to use theory critically in order that she may posit a full feminine sexuality and a language that would be adequate to the feminine imaginary. In this context she stresses that the psychoanalytic account of the male and female body are symbiotic. The masculine body is dependent on the feminine body for its present morphological form, that is, for its phallic attributes. By writing about a feminine body that is not the inverse or the complement of the male body she presents a challenge to masculinity, as it is presently constructed, by exposing its covert dependence on the patriarchally constructed feminine morphology.

Clearly, this kind of approach takes us a long way from the Anglo-American difference vs. equality debate, at the same time as it by-passes the issue of essentialism. There is no essence on this view: there is the social, the historical and the future to be lived/created. And as for the issue of equality, this always involves, for Irigaray, a question of reducing difference to the same: the one subject, the essentially human, which is to say the ahistorical and implicitly male subject of philosophy. All this would achieve is that women could 'become-men' – a ploy that leaves phallocentrism intact and strengthened. Both equality and the reversal of values are out of the question as both quickly reduce to *following the law of the same*: difference would again be levelled to the norm, the male standard.[59] Rather we need to struggle for a social organization and a way of thinking and speaking where both men and women can live the specificity of their bodies and their desires. This would involve putting woman's body into language and the end of the domination of the phallus in language and culture. It would involve the articulation of (an)other economy of thought in which plurality and multiplicity could have positive value. As she concludes in 'Women's Exile':

> It would be necessary for women to be recognized as bodies with sexual attributes, desiring and uttering, and for men to rediscover the materiality of their bodies. There should no longer be this separation: sex/language on the one hand; body/matter on the other. Then, perhaps another history would be possible . . .[60]

In particular it would make possible a *relation* between the sexes, a relation of two presences, not one and its complement. Perhaps then we could consider heterosexual relations on a model other than rape,[61] where the male breaks into a body on which there is 'nothing to see' because, for him, there is 'nothing there'. Perhaps then women too would have a desire, a presence, rather than the passive option of inviting the penis-child to take up residence in its 'old home', the vagina-womb.

Cixous seems to share this sense of an other economy when she claims:

> Things are starting to be written, things that will constitute a feminine Imaginary, the site, that is, of identifications of an ego no longer given over to an image defined by the masculine.[62]

The return of the feminine from its repression may well be one way of understanding the explosion of women's writing that the last quarter of this century is witnessing. Perhaps contemporary culture no longer requires the repression or the repudiation of femininity to ensure its integrity. Or, perhaps, its own integrity is in such tatters that the return of its repressions is one of many symptoms of its 'madness'. In either case, the 'break[ing] down' of the coherence of Western culture may be prerequisite to reassembling in a more viable and polyvalent form.

The next, and final, chapter will consider another kind of 'body' whose construction has much in common with the phallocentricity of the (male) individual: the body politic.

7

Sexual Difference or Sexual Equality?

In the introduction, it was suggested that the mind/body, reason/passion and nature/culture dichotomies interact with the male/female dichotomy in extremely complex ways, often prejudicial to women. What has been shown in the ensuing chapters is the way that these dichotomies function in the work of particular philosophers and the consequences of this functioning for their views on sexual difference. It has become apparent in the course of this analysis that in contemporary thought it is the private/public distinction which organizes these dualisms and gives them their distinctively sexually specific character. The private, domestic sphere purports to be concerned with *natural* relations: relations between the sexes, relations between parents and children and human reproduction. It has a particular concern with *bodies*, with their reproduction, regeneration and recuperation. The private sphere is also the realm of the *passions*: sexual passion and the satisfaction or management of human emotive needs. In socio-economic terms, the private sphere is constructed as the realm of consumption, whereas the public sphere is constructed as the realm of production and exchange. The public sphere is regulated by relations of exchange between individuals who are defined by their relation to the market: buyer of labour, seller of labour, owner of products, and so on. These relations are conceived as *artificial* or *cultural* and as involving *rational* decisions and interactions which override any pre-political relations that one may have had with nature.

Much of the cultural and conceptual complexity of the way human life is presently organized stems from this dichotomy between the private and the public spheres and the overriding sexual specification of these two spheres of activity. The difficulty of disentangling women's subjectivity from the private sphere – even *conceptually* – can be accounted for by this intricate and extensive cross-referencing of the private sphere with the body, passions and nature. Likewise, to attempt the full insertion of women into the public sphere, equitably and *as women*, involves grappling with the practical and conceptual oppositions between the construction of their subjectivity in the private sphere and the kind of subjectivity that is appropriate to the relations characteristic of the public sphere. The attempt to reconceptualize the private and the public spheres is obstructed by these interlocking and intersupporting distinctions. One cannot, then, rethink women's social role and status without also rethinking our conceptions of nature, passion and the body.

It has been suggested that it is to the detriment of much feminist theorizing that it treats these dichotomies as ontologically given. I argued that the opposing views of de Beauvoir and Firestone, on one hand, and McMillan, on the other, have more in common than it would seem. In particular, it was argued that they share a dualist conception of human life: one in which the mind is opposed to the body, the individual to its 'natural' function and culture to nature. The major difference between these two views, I argued, is a difference in the *evaluation* of our cultural situation rather than a difference in what that situation is taken to be. The debate between them then becomes whether or not to 'choose' to apply artificial measures in order to alter what is understood as a natural (or bodily) inequality. I have tried to show, in the course of this study, that the 'choice' between an artificially achieved *equality* between the sexes or the maintenance of a natural *difference* between the sexes is one that remains within a paradigm of thought which is entrenched in modern philosophy, so much so that this 'choice' appears to be exclusive and exhaustive. In this chapter I will sketch out some of the consequences for political thought and action of being constrained by this 'choice'. In the brief conclusion I point to the need for an entirely different approach to the problems of reconceptualizing female subjectivity and its socio-political possibilities.

1 From Nature to Political Culture

Recent feminist theorists have elaborated the way in which political theorists, particularly in the modern period, have claimed that the political body is a product of the fertility of men joined in the name of their love for reason, order and justice.[1] Whether pre-political society is conceived as a primitive social state or as a state of isolated individuals in nature, the passage to political society is consistently represented as a passage undertaken by men only. The conditions under which passions and needs are satisfied are transformed by socio-political relations and this transformation is taken to reflect the triumph of reason, foresight and deferral. Men in the state of nature may also, reluctantly, be attracted to each other through fear. Fear is the motivation which Hobbes stresses in his account of how men come to create the 'artificial man', or leviathan. He writes:

> [B]y art is created that great LEVIATHAN called a COMMONWEALTH, or STATE, in Latin CIVITAS, which is but an artificial man; though of greater stature and strength than the natural, for whose protection and defence it was intended; and in which the *sovereignty* is an artificial *soul*, as giving motion and life to the whole body; the *magistrates*, and other *officers* of judicature and execution, artificial *joints*; *reward* and *punishment*, by which fastened to the seat of the sovereignty every joint and member is moved to perform his duty, are the *nerves*, that do the same in the body natural; and *wealth* and *riches* of all the particular members are the *strength*; *salus populi*, the people's safety, its *business*; *counsellors*, by whom all things needful for it to know are suggested unto it, are the *memory*; *equity* and *laws*, an artificial *reason* and *will*; *concord, health*; *sedition, sickness*; and civil war, death. Lastly, the *pacts* and *covenants*, by which the parts of this body politic were at first made, set together, and united, resemble that *fiat*, or the *let us make man*, pronounced by God in the creation.[2]

Several points need to be made in relation to this view. First, it is God who makes man, and man who, in turn, makes political life. Woman is absent. God has usurped her reproductive power to create 'men' and she is not a creator, nor even a co-creator, of the political body. Hence there is no feminine leviathan, no artificial woman, 'though of greater stature and strength than the natural', who can protect and defend natural woman. In relation to the body politic woman is left unprotected, undefended, virtually in the state of nature where, according to Hobbes, one dwells in 'continual fear' and in 'danger of violent death'.[3]

Woman is incorporated into the political body, though not by contract or pact. Her status is not so different from the status of those whom Hobbes describes as accepting, by word or deed, that they have been conquered by war.[4] By submitting to such conquest these beings are henceforth *bound to obey* the laws of a body that they had no part in forming.[5] The metaphor of the 'artificial man' functions in political theory to achieve two important effects. First, it constructs the sphere of political and civil relations as relations between *male* bodies. This construction has consequences for women's political and ethical status. The leviathan incorporates and so controls women's bodies in a manner which does not infringe upon the artificial man's claim to autonomy, since her contributions are neither acknowledged nor visible as socio-political contributions. They are taken for granted as part of the *natural* foundation for political life, not as part of it. If the political body did represent female as well as male bodies, then, presumably, women would not be confined to the 'natural' roles of wife/mother, but would also be eligible to be sisters in a civic sorority. Given that there are/were no such sororities, women have/had little choice but to avail themselves of the 'protection' that joining themselves to a husband provides. David Hume comes close to acknowledging this state of affairs. He describes these male corporations as 'confederacies' and observes that:

> though the males, *when united*, have in all countries *bodily force* sufficient to maintain [this] severe tyranny, yet such are the *insinuation, address* and *charms* of their fair companions, that women are commonly able to break the *confederacy*, and share with the other sex in all the rights and privileges of society.[6]

Significantly, these comments are made alongside the judgement that 'we' are not under any obligation to extend to 'barbarous Indians' the rules of justice, nor are 'they' entitled to the possession of rights and property. Again, if these beings enter the body politic, either by being 'imported' as slaves or by the conquest of their lands, they are incorporated into the body politic without alteration to the image of that body politic. This is important because in so far as the artificial man can maintain his unity through incorporation, he is not required to acknowledge difference. The metaphor of the body politic has functioned in the history of Western societies to restrict the political vocabulary to one voice only: a voice that speaks of only *one* body, *one* reason and *one* ethic. If these 'other' beings attempt to speak to that body their speech is not recognized. When Wollstonecraft, for example, addressed the political body to speak of women's rights, Walpole called not only her womanhood but also her humanity into question, by dubbing her the 'hyena in petticoats'. Likewise Burke called the women who spoke to the unstable French body politic, during the revolution, the 'furies from hell'. Even J. S. Mill infantilizes those colonized by the British, by describing them as still in their 'nonage'.

In contemporary times, bodies politic more commonly incorporate 'others' by *assimilation*. Nevertheless, the problem remains of what these 'others' can say of their 'otherness' from *within* the body politic and using the language of that body politic. In Australia this problem is revealed in the way in which Aborigines, if they wish to be heard, are compelled to articulate their claims and their original occupancy of the continent in terms of land *rights* and *ownership*. These terms are appropriate to the relationship which the colonizers have to land, but inappropriate to Aborigines' traditional relationship to land.[7] This is to say that the body politic admits only those who can 'speak its language' or, at least, who can *mime* its reason and its ethics, in its voice. In relation to women's occupation of the public, political sphere, that sphere continues to assume that its members are free from the tasks of reproduction and domestic work. The female body is publicly acknowledged only in so far as it agrees with the 'whisperings' of the Hobbesian counsellors and 'wills' the same laws.

2 Labour, Property and Contracts

Traditionally, the character and legitimacy of political society is accounted for by the interplay of three terms: labour, property and contracts. The particular configuration of these terms varies from theorist to theorist,[8] yet the terms themselves are consistently defined in ways that exclude women from political society. The security of the results of labour and the stabilization of property are guaranteed by the establishment of laws or contracts which govern production and exchange. *Every* man, it is supposed, has something to gain from these arrangements since 'every Man has a *Property* in his own *person* . . .'[9] Moreover, since it is only in political society that genuine human freedom[10] is realized, women are excluded not only from socially constituted proprietorial relations, they are also excluded from this realm of socio-political freedom.

The labour of women, the very *person* of woman, involves other relations. In the transition from pre-political to political society, she remains bound to 'natural' familial relations. Engels hypothesizes the character of this aspect of women's being in the following way:

> In the old communistic household, which embraced numerous couples and their children, the administration of the household, entrusted to the women, was just as much a public, a socially necessary industry as the providing of food by the men. This situation changed with the patriarchal family, and even more with the monogamous individual family. The administration of the household lost its public character. It was no longer the concern of society. *It became a private service.*[11]

But, does not this 'private' service assume a 'public' which it is defined against? This privatization of women's labour could not be prior to labour-conceived-as-property relations. For the household to lose its 'public character' production itself must have already left the home, 'embodied' in the figure of the labourer. In this case can it be an *a priori* truth of woman that 'the labour of her body and the work of her hands are not properly hers'? How else can one make sense of the logic of woman's relation to man?

[I]n marriage the wife differs from the ordinary courtesan only in that she does not hire out her body, like a wage-worker, on piece-work, but sells it into slavery once for all.[12]

Clearly, women's bodies are not conceptualized as capable of providing goods or objects suitable for exchange. Objections to this view were offered in chapter 6, where the work of Cixous and Irigaray was discussed. On the liberal view, there is a prior claim on women's bodies/capacities that tie them to nature and to a natural order, which precludes them from participating in the social order. The products of women's labour fall outside the scope of public production and women, along with the family, are ironically cast as the consumers of the productiveness of the public sphere. And if 'the *value*, or *worth* of a man, is as of all other things, his price; that is to say, so much as would be given for the use of his power',[13] what could be the value or worth of one who gives away, 'once and for all' her power to labour?

Thus, it would seem that from the beginnings of the capitalist era women are conceptualized as *naturally* unsuited to the production of social value and hence as falling outside the body politic. Even on the most severe of the early modern accounts of the legitimate polity, 'the liberty to buy, and sell, and otherwise contract with one another'[14] was not denied to the *subject* of a Commonwealth. This liberty was not encroached upon even by the *absolute* sovereign. Yet, any or every man could command the labour of a woman. Husbands, as representatives of the body politic in the private sphere, were vested with authority in relation to the household and its members. Women were thus not conceptualized as having a governing relation to themselves or any obligation to the body politic but rather were constituted as the *objects* of a 'natural' governing relation. The major ethical requirement made on them by the body politic was that they be obedient and chaste. Women thus come to symbolize, or literally embody, the natural, the familial and the domestic. The full significance of the bodily differences between men and women were constructed in this division between the private and public spheres of social life. In the former, natural human functions and needs were attended to by women. To a large extent this remains the means by which such needs are managed. In the latter, artificially created contractual obligations and relations obtain between men and also women, but not under the same conditions.

Rousseau, among others, urges that these differences are fundamental to the establishment of civilization. Moreover, the continued existence of these sexual differences is fundamental to the operations and continuance of civilization. Rousseau would disagree with Mill's view that human progress dictates the erosion of these first relations. To bear children, to nurture both husband and children and to provide the base for socio-political relations between men are among the tasks that Rousseau assigns to women. To erode these fundamental relations, he supposes, would be to erode civilization itself. It is men only, on his account, who make the transition from natural to socio-political relations. Women remain tied to nature. They provide the backdrop to the stage of social life, yet are never permitted to act on it.

Rousseau, like Hobbes and Locke, does not count women's labour and its products as capable of constituting proprietorial relations. Recall the explanation he offers Emile of his relation to the results of his labour. The expenditure of his time, his labour and his trouble give him title to the land upon which he has worked, as much so as if it were 'a part of himself'.[15] Needless to say, the time, labour, trouble and self Sophy invests in her work is treated quite differently. In her case, it creates no such claims on the objects/subjects of her work, nor any right to prevent the appropriation of her work by another. Paradoxically, in her case, it is often the very object/subject of her labour who appropriates her labour, that is, who literally 'consumes' it in the very *process* of its expression.

The human subject which is capable of becoming a political subject is implicitly a male person. He is one whose subjectivity entails, but cannot be *reduced to*, a capacity to transform nature in the production of socially valuable, that is, *exchangeable*, goods. His subjectivity cannot be reduced to this capacity because this capacity is alienable. The capacity to labour, to create and transform, is itself an exchangeable power not synonymous with the subject. Marx, the most significant critic of the liberal social order, bases his critique on the identification of (male) subjectivity with this capacity to labour on and hence transform nature.[16] The subject compelled to alienate his capacity to labour, and therefore the products of his labour, is an alienated subject. Communism proposes to restore man to himself by the abolition of private property and wage labour. Marx is, however, curiously silent concerning woman's subjectivity and its relation to nature. Marxist/feminists have argued that Marxist political theory needs to take account of the alienation of women's labour that occurs in the *absence* of a wage relation.[17] The problem that woman's subjectivity poses to the liberal paradigm can also be posed to the Marxist paradigm. In order to delve further into this obvious peculiarity of female nature it is necessary to consider the asymmetrical relations that women, on one hand, and men, on the other, have to sexuality, subjectivity and reproduction.

3 Sexuality, Subjectivity and Reproduction

An implicit assumption in the history of the theorization of the relations between reason/passion, mind/body and nature/culture is that men are able to dissociate themselves from sexuality, reproduction and natural passions. Male subjectivity and male sexuality are able to be divorced conceptually and spatially ('man is only man now and again') in a way that female subjectivity and female sexuality are not ('but the female is always a female').[18] Since it is she who has been allotted the role of perpetuating and managing the 'natural' base of culture, she cannot be considered independently of these functions, which coincide in traditional accounts, with her sexuality. The satisfaction and management of the needs of natural man – 'food, a female, shelter' – have become the work of women. She tends to the needs of 'natural man' whilst he is transforming himself into 'social man'.

Any attempt to introduce women into the body politic raises, necessarily, the question of how these 'natural' human needs are to be satisfied. The social reduction of woman to her function of satisfying these needs makes it conceptually impossible to consider her *social* possibilities without also considering, as a social problem, the question of the reproduction of the natural base of cultural life. To insist on the radical social equality of women involves rejecting, as necessary, the natural organization of the natural basis of culture. Of the traditional political theorists, Mill comes closest to approaching this position. He argues in favour of the progressive amendment of nature by rational social intervention. However, as was argued in chapter 2, Mill is still faced with the problems of human reproduction, infant dependence and domestic labour. The very strong distinction which he maintains between the private life of the individual and the public life of the citizen exposes the dualist notion he has of public socio-political relations and private familial/sexual relations. His concern with protecting the private sphere of thought, personal taste and private relations from the intrusions of the government forecloses the possibility of challenging the 'private' arrangements between men and women. The labour, effort and 'self' of women are contained in the private sphere, where they are 'protected' from public scrutiny, and where structural inequalities between the inhabitants (husbands and wives, fathers and children) are rendered socially and politically invisible. This state of affairs is much to the disadvantage of women and children. It creates the social space in which husbands/fathers can abuse wives and children with little fear of state interference: domestic violence and rape/incest are cases in point.

Mill baulks at the point at which a consistent liberal view would require the application of Locke's principles of labour and property to the private 'contracts' made between men and women.[19] To effect the total insertion of women into capitalist society would involve the acknowledgement of the 'blind spot' of traditional socio-political theorizing: that the reproduction of the species, sexual relations and domestic work are performed under *socially constructed* conditions, not natural ones, and that these tasks are socially and economically necessary. In contemporary Western life the widespread availability of reliable contraception has introduced practical options for many women that Mill was only able to hypothesize. The 'choice' of motherhood and/or career that was unrealistic in Mill's time has become, at least for some women, a viable option. This is an aspect of modern life on which feminists have been quick to capitalize.

Both de Beauvoir and Firestone, for example, argue that science can free women from the historical conflation of their subjectivity, sexuality and reproductive capacity. These theorists see culture as offering the possibility of transcending or progressively rejecting the natural basis of culture and argue that this possibility *should* be actualized. De Beauvoir takes this advance of civilization to be sufficient to allow the rebuttal of the traditional reductive description of women: 'Tota mulier in utero.'[20] Woman can now be woman 'only now and again'. This opens up the possibility of actualizing an old dream in which a sex-neutral human consciousness commands a tractable body-machine. What was merely a theoretical difficulty for Mill has become, in our contemporary context, an urgent practical problem. What is to become of all that has, at least since the early eighteenth century, been associated with women? Sensuality, child-rearing and domestic work are still aspects of human life that require management. In a liberal capitalist society the obvious response is to put them 'on the market' as objects of negotiation and contracts. These 'natural', private aspects of human life thus come into relations of exchange with other aspects of social and economic life.[21]

Mill's disembodied, 'in principle' equality which, I argued, embodied women cannot actualize may be superseded by an 'embodied' equality once women's private containment in nature is overcome, that is, once the body comes under the rational control of science. Putting the body, its needs, desires and 'private' pleasures on the market, and subjecting it to utilitarian principles of maximum pleasure at minimum cost and pain, suggests social and sexual relations from which many recoil. The issues raised by this possibility are among the most debated and dismal in current feminist literature. The tentative attempts, by both de Beauvoir and Firestone, to describe what woman's subjectivity – liberated from reproduction – may be like, are the most unsatisfactory parts of their texts.

It is a striking peculiarity of much contemporary feminist writing that the essential component of female subjectivity, once it is freed from the 'tyranny' of nature, is taken to be female sexuality. Michel Foucault offers an analysis of the tendency inherent in modern Western culture 'to direct the question of what we are, to sex'.[22] In the context of contemporary feminist theory, directing 'the question of what we are to sex' is an indication of the uncritical interaction that much feminist theory has with cultural constructions of female subjectivity. I have argued that this construction reduces women's subjectivity to her sexuality which in turn is understood to coincide with her reproductive capacity. If the reproductive capacity of women can be mastered, what we are left with is woman's subjectivity as defined by her sexuality, which is now open for reconstruction. It is the question of what to make of women's sexuality in the future society that comes to dominate the accounts of female subjectivity offered by de Beauvoir and Firestone.

In the penultimate chapter of *The Second Sex*, entitled 'The Independent Woman', de Beauvoir turns her attention to the possibilities of future woman. Significantly, much of what she has to say there concerns relations between the sexes. If family life, along with the responsibilities and shared interests that it engenders, is no longer central to the relations between men and women, on what will their future interactions be based? De Beauvoir seems to argue that shared projects, of a non-familial nature, are essential to future male/female interactions. The most obvious remaining tie between men and women is the sphere of sensuality. De Beauvoir is not optimistic about the possibility of an equitable or shared male/female eroticism. She rejects 'casual encounters' between the sexes since relations between strangers are 'relations that are on a plane of brutality'[23] in which women are particularly prone to risk their physical well-being. She also rejects the notion that women may take a lover 'as a man often takes a mistress'.[24] This 'financial' arrangement will be unsatisfactory for a woman since she is aware of the indignity of this arrangement, for both parties. Satisfying relations between the sexes, she argues, assume an equality of capability, of desire and of intent. Yet, even those men who willingly acknowledge intellectual equality, are not ready to treat even the 'exceptional' woman as an equal in the sphere of eroticism. The options available to the independent woman are bleak. Either she can take refuge in a masochism intrinsic to the structure of *feminine* sexuality, where she may be glad to relinquish the control she otherwise maintains. Or she may assert what de Beauvoir calls a 'virile independence' that will often lead to disappointment and failure, since most men are not up to this show of female activity.

Firestone's attempts to grope towards a liberated sexuality seem more simple, if not simplistic. For her, all humans, in the context of cybernetic communism, would have a 'free' sexuality. Here, the possibility of the complete artificialization, and hence socialization, of human reproduction involves the literal neutering of all bodies. The child's body, no less than the female's body, can come into relations of exchange with any other body since all are reduced to the same in an economy based on pleasure rather than reproduction. In this economy,

[i]t is possible that the child might form his first close physical relationships with people his own size out of sheer physical convenience, just as men and

women, all else being equal, might prefer each other over those of the same
sex for sheer physical fit . . . [!]
Relations with children would include as much genital sex as the child was
capable of – probably considerably more than we now believe . . .[25]

The possibilities of a future liberated sexuality are here based on calculations of bodily mechanics and their possible combinations. Differences of
age and sex are reduced to the mechanics of a circulation governed by the
phallus that echoes the writings of one even less popular with feminists
than Firestone presently is: the Marquis de Sade.

Finally, it should be noted that neither de Beauvoir nor Firestone
offer any serious consideration of non-heterosexual relations. Presumably, if women are no longer dependent – economically, socially or
reproductively – on men, heterosexuality will no longer be an obvious
or 'automatic' choice for women. Rich has explored this issue in 'Compulsory Heterosexuality and Lesbian Existence', pointing out that '[h]etero-
sexuality has been both forcibly and subliminally imposed on women. Yet
everywhere women have resisted it, often at the cost of physical torture,
imprisonment, psychosurgery, social ostracism, and extreme poverty.'[26]
Although Rich is careful to stress that the issue of lesbian existence cannot
be reduced to 'who one sleeps with', she nevertheless does use the issue of
female sexuality as the definitive component in women's identity. In view
of Foucault's comments concerning 'Les bijoux indiscrets',[27] feminists need
to be more critical of this tendency to reduce women's identity to their
sexuality. This is, after all, precisely what historically dominant discourses on women have done. In particular, more attention should be
drawn to the way in which discourses on sexuality define heterosexuality
and homosexuality interdependently.

4   Sexual Equality and Freedom on the Open Market

The extremes of sexual equality and sexual difference were in fact
sketched out long ago: in the work of de Sade and Rousseau, respectively.
De Sade, a great admirer of Rousseau, nevertheless departs from his views
on sexual difference. De Sade takes the principles of liberal political
theory into that most private place of the private sphere: the bedroom.
Consider his views in the following passage in relation to the views of
Hobbes, Locke and Rousseau on labour and property.

Since, however, the torch of philosophy has dissipated all those impostures,
since, the celestial chimera has been tumbled in the dust, since, better
instructed of physic's laws and secrets, we have evolved the principle of

generation, and now that this material mechanism offers nothing more astonishing to the eye than the development of a germ of wheat, we have been called back to Nature and away from human error. As we have broadened the horizons of our rights, we have recognized that we are perfectly free to take back what we only gave up reluctantly, or by accident, and that it is impossible to demand of any individual whomsoever that he become a father or a mother against his will; that this creature whether more or less on earth is not of very much consequence, and that we become, in a word, as certainly the masters of this morsel of flesh, however it be animated, as we are of the nails we pare from our fingers, or the excrements we eliminate through our bowels, *because the one and the other are our own, and because we are absolute proprietors of what emanates from us.*[28]

Just as we cannot force a man to labour against his will, de Sade argues, we cannot compel a man, or a woman, into parenthood. The Lockean principles of proprietorship that apply to man's body and its products can apply to woman's body and its products. Once the mysteries of nature are unveiled to reveal nothing more than a sophisticated material mechanism, our moral sentiments prove to be little more than superstition. De Sade's writings, particularly *Philosophy in the Bedroom*, anticipate in stark form many of the sentiments of later theorizing around the body, reproduction and sexuality. Presumably, he would be one of those who, in our current context, would argue that 'baby-selling', or surrogate motherhood, is the exclusive concern of the seller of the product of her body and the buyer.

Rousseau and de Sade together can be taken to represent the outer limits of a paradigm intrinsic to modern sexual/political theory. Rousseau offers us an account of sexual *difference* within this paradigm that places woman *outside* the body politic, as its ground and support. She does not work or transform or exchange with others but rather repeats, indefinitely and under static conditions, the ground of culture. She creates and sustains biological boys who will be 'born again' into culture as citizens and free labourers, and biological girls who will remain in nature to replace their mothers. De Sade offers an account of sexual *equality* where women are fully admitted, where they are *inside* the cultural sphere and governed by the same laws of equivalence and exchange as men. The Sadian woman 'becomes a man'. In de Sade's sexual economy the phallus circulates freely between the sexes. Women wear dildos, 'encunt' quite as often as they are penetrated, 'ejaculate' along with men and despise motherhood. De Sade represents these two types, the woman of difference and the woman of equality, in the characters of Justine and Juliette. The respective fortunes of these heroines make it quite clear which of the two is going to profit within the prevailing socio-economic system.[29]

Rousseau's Sophy or Julie is easily recognized in the pathetic but ever virtuous figure of Justine – the title of de Sade's text, *La Nouvelle Justine*, deliberately echoes that of Rousseau's *La Nouvelle Héloïse*. It is Juliette, the woman who has achieved equality and integration, who knows her 'cash value', who both thrives and wins the respect of men. De Sade's work raises an important issue that confronts us now: can there be, in our present context, a 'liberated' female sexuality that is distinct from a libertine's sexuality? How can women's entrenchment in the private sphere of reproduction, childrearing, sexuality and relations between the sexes be overcome without subjecting these aspects of human life to their 'cash value'?

One does not have to lapse into the romantic humanism of McMillan to take issue with the sexual 'equality' of future woman as envisaged here. Yet the alternative vision of de Beauvoir's' 'independent woman' or Firestone's 'cybernetic communism' are no more attractive constructions of a possible future that, one suspects, de Sade has captured more realistically. The means available to us to conceptualize culture and the form of our culture itself make it very difficult to see beyond this choice: either respect for nature and woman's *difference* within it; or the desire to dominate or transcend nature to effect women's *equality* in culture. In this chapter I have tried to show that both these strategies belong to the same problematic. The disjunctive difference/equality impasse reflects the problems involved in a dualistic understanding of the body and nature, on the one hand, and consciousness and culture on the other.

We can begin to address this impasse by taking issue with what equality for women could mean in the present social, political and economic context. Again, the liberal tradition, in spite of itself, captures the dilemma clearly. Taylor's recommendations concerning the emancipation of women were treated, along with those of Mill, in chapter 2. Unlike Mill, she stressed the necessity for the full integration of women into wage labour. She argues that,

> [s]o long as competition is the general law of human life, it is tyranny to shut out one-half of the competitors. All who have attained the age of self-government have an equal claim to be permitted *to sell whatever kind of useful labour they are capable of, for the price which it will bring.*[30]

Taylor acknowledges perhaps more than she realizes here. Useful labour is determined 'by the market' as is 'the price which it will bring'. The introduction of women into a historically male-dominated economy is prejudiced by what 'the market' takes the useful labour of women to be. The historical conditions of the sexual division of labour means that when women enter the labour market they carry the private sphere with them. If the choice is between servicing the public in general or servicing a particular man/household, many women will continue to prefer the latter. Interestingly enough even this 'choice' is becoming an unreal one to middle-, as well as working-class, women. Many women today have both 'the boss' at home *and* the boss at work to contend with. The confusion in the (female-dominated) service and secretarial industries, concerning the hidden job description is well documented in feminist sociological studies.[31] Occupations that are female-dominated are overwhelmingly analogous to the tasks of mothers/wives/housewives, that is, to the type of work women have traditionally performed in the private sphere. Many jobs require of women those skills which are stereotypically associated with the wife's role, for example, tension management, submissiveness and, far too often, sexual availability.

One may find it difficult to distinguish between the Sadian and liberal views of equality. Angela Carter's reflections on the morality of de Sade, for example, may equally count as a reflection on Taylor's proposition. Carter asks:

[i]f the world in its present state is indeed a brothel – and the moral difference between *selling one's sexual labour and one's manual labour* is, in these terms, . . . an academic one – then every attempt the individual makes to escape the conditions of sale will only bring a girl back to the crib, again, in some form or another.[32]

The problem is that women's 'sexual labour' and women's 'manual labour' are conceptually and historically so intertwined that they are not easily separated. This is both a conceptual and a practical problem in the present conditions of women's lives. An alternative mode of conceptualizing the diversity and richness of human activity and interactions that does not reduce all socially valuable and socially necessary activity to market relations is essential if we are to pose alternative ways of living. A politico-ethical language and practice that is neither wholly dependent on nor wholly inappropriate to present socio-economic relations would also need to be developed.

Conclusion

Under present conditions of social and political life our means of conceptualizing alternative arrangements seem scarce. One is led back again and again, irrespective of one's theoretical starting point, to the 'choice' between a sexual difference whose origin is located outside culture (Rousseau, McMillan), and to the construction of a sexual equality within culture (Mill, de Beauvoir, Firestone). What is conceptually and practically possible is tied to the present conditions of our lives in such a way that it is difficult to see how one could change present socio-political, economic and ethical relations. Our social practices and our reflections on them seem to run on an unbroken and circular path. Breaking into this self-justifying system requires both that we confront those points of tension and contradiction in our own lives and that we draw on resources other than those employed in traditional socio-political theory. The great diversity, characteristic of contemporary urban life in terms of race, values and beliefs, can be seen as conducive to a radical reassessment of how we live in socio-political communities.[1]

This is not meant to suggest that the way we live is completely determined by the ideas that we hold and live by, whether consciously or unconsciously. Obviously political struggles around economic, legal, social and political arrangements are absolutely crucial to social change. However, it is to suggest that writing, speaking and thinking about alternative ways of understanding human being, sexual difference and socio-political life *are* themselves forms of political struggle. Women, and other groups, have historically had far too little to say in relation to these crucial issues. Women speaking in public, of women, is clearly a threat to the integrity of the political body – as the comments of Walpole and Burke demonstrate.

In chapter 5 it was argued that feminist theory can not theorize in a void, 'outside' of patriarchal thought and relations. Feminist theory has at its disposal, however, a much richer store of thought than that represented in the present dominant paradigm. In particular, the history of philosophy has a much richer store of conceptions of the body, passion and nature than appears in liberal accounts.[2] I have argued that the traditional oppositions between the mind and body, reason and passion, culture and nature, are oppositions that work against offering a dynamic account of female subjectivity and its possibilities. Whilst we continue to accept the dominant descriptions of nature, passion or emotion and the body, we are also committed to the circular and self-justifying track upon which they run, including women's embodiment of the dominated half of these dualisms. These oppositions run through the work of Rousseau, Wollstonecraft, Mill, Taylor, de Beauvoir, McMillan and Daly. It was argued in chapter 6 that psychoanalytic theory and aspects of French feminist thought contribute to the development of non-dualistic conceptions of human being. Some Australian and Anglo-American feminist writing is also relevant here.[3] Clearly, the equality versus difference debate is not reducible to a debate between Anglo-American and French feminisms. This way of thinking about the equality/difference debate remains caught up within a binary problematic.

One of the most important areas in which women, and others who have been politically marginalized, need to contribute is that of reconceptualizing our politico-ethical lives. I have argued that the political body, formed by the social contract, has been explicitly a masculine body. Women's bodies also need to be represented, both symbolically and in fact, if our body politic is to become one capable of genuinely ethical relations. It is therefore necessary to begin the task of addressing how *different* bodies occupy the 'pre-defined' positions and the 'pre-constituted' points of power or authority as these are laid out in Hobbes's description of the artificial man. Some consideration needs to be given to *how*, or in what manner, different bodies occupy the *same* social space *differently*.

Lloyd has shown, in another context, that it is not so much that women are explicitly conceptualized as irrational but rather that rationality itself is defined against the 'womanly'. In this context it may be profitable to explore the linked genealogies of the 'sex-neutral' modern human subject and the 'sex-neutral' modern body politic. Woman's relation to the 'modern body politic' has features in common with her relation to the 'modern human subject': both are the invention of modern philosophical discourses. The point is that although women have been described as unsuited to political participation,[4] political participation has itself been defined in such a way that it excludes women's bodies. Struggling to have women included in the present body politic is therefore counterproductive unless it is accompanied by some analysis of the exclusions which operate on women's corporeality.

The work of Foucault may prove useful in this context. He completely rejects the idea that the body has a fixed character which sets the limits of possible socio-political structures in which that body could 'live'. He inverts the modern problematic and questions instead how socio-political structures construct particular kinds of bodies, with particular powers/ capacities, needs and desires. Yet, Foucault has little to say concerning the patriarchal character of modern political life. This leads to a 'blind spot' in his own theorizations of power. It may well be, as he claims, that no one body can seize power or exercise power from a single locus. It is nonethe-less clearly the case that under existing arrangements different *types* of bodies can utilize positions of power more effectively than others. Of this he has little to say. A satisfactory analysis of this issue would involve addressing politics from the standpoint of entrenched bodily dif-ferences, such as sexual difference. In turn, this would inevitably raise moral and ethical issues.

Recently several philosophers have acknowledged that there is a 'crisis' in contemporary moral life and theory. Alasdair MacIntyre, for example, acknowledges that there is no obvious way, in contemporary moral life, to settle contrary moral claims. He has little to say on the connections between politics and ethics but in the postscript to the second edition of *After Virtue* he asserts that

> [m]oral philosophies, however they may aspire to achieve more than this, always do articulate the morality of some particular social and cultural standpoint: Aristotle is the spokesman for one class of fourth century Athenians, Kant . . . provides a rational voice for the emerging social forces of liberal individualism.[5]

MacIntyre acknowledges here that ethics has historically been the product of whichever group has monopolized political right: Greek (male) citizens or the liberal (male) individual. Clearly, part of the privilege accorded to members of a political body is that their needs, desires and powers are converted into rights and virtues. The alleged equity of universalizing ethical principles that were developed from a particular historical and political perspective is one of many indications of the arrogance of Western moral philosophy.

In place of the attempts to universalize the values of white, male heads of households, an ethics that takes account of historical, social, ethnic and bodily differences needs to be developed. This, in turn, requires that the dream of the unified *one* body of Hobbes's artificial man be abandoned. Throughout this book I have been concerned with constructions of woman, femininity and the female body in modern philosophical thought. For that reason I have stressed woman's relation to the (masculine) political body. It is not my aim, however, to pronounce the fiat 'let there be woman' and entrench the historical construction of dualistically conceived sexual difference. The political body, no less than the individualized body, with which it is complicit, must be acknowledged as polymorphous.

If there is to be a genuinely polymorphous socio-political body, it is clear that it will need to be capable of discriminating and respecting differences among its members. This would involve institutionalizing the ability to *contextualize* actions and their meanings rather than taking a *relativist* stance toward issues of ethics. It also implies the ability to hear and respond to polyvocality and polyvalency. Part of what is involved in the viability of such a body is that its communication with itself would be polylogical. This would not amount to each member, whether an individual or a group, deciding for itself its moral codes, since each member must be able to interact with other individual or group members of the larger body. An individual's membership in any particular group would not exclude her or him from other groups. Hence, the mobility of any particular individual may serve to draw links between a variety of groups.

Of course, this notion of a polylogical, polymorphous socio-political body is vague and it is beyond the scope of this work to engage with it in any detail. What is in order to stress here is that it is crucial to begin thinking of ways in which those excluded from current systems of political representation may be represented in present and future conceptions of socio-political and ethical life, represented both *symbolically* and in fact. Such representation must avoid privileging historically valued human powers and capacities over powers and capacities that have been repressed or distorted.[6] Perhaps then the great diversity in current moral, social and political life may be viewed as potential strengths rather than presenting the threat of chaos or anarchy.

Notes

INTRODUCTION

1 For example, J. Mitchell, *Psychoanalysis and Feminism*, Penguin, Harmondsworth, 1974; J. Gallop, *Feminism and Psychoanalysis: The Daughter's Seduction*, MacMillan Press, London, 1982.

2 For example, B. Weinbaum, *The Curious Courtship of Feminism and Socialism*, South End Press, Boston, 1978; M. Barrett, *Women's Oppression Today: Problems in Marxist Feminist Analysis*, Verso, London, 1980.

3 A worthwhile contribution to this problem is S. Harding, ed., *Feminism and Methodology*, Indiana University Press, Bloomington, 1987; see, especially, introduction and conclusion.

4 Chapters 1, 2, 3, 6 and 7 consider feminist uses of these philosophies.

5 For example, the extensive use made of so-called 'oppression and liberation theorists' by the 1970s feminist movement: see P. Freire, *Pedagogy of the Oppressed*, Penguin, Harmondsworth, 1974; A. Memmi, *The Colonizer and the Colonized*, Beacon Press, Boston, 1972. These analyses were made use of in such works as A. Summers, *Damned Whores and God's Police: The Colonization of Women in Australia*, Pelican, Harmondsworth, 1975.

6 See H. Hartmann, 'The Unhappy Marriage of Marxism and Feminism: Towards a More Progressive Union', *Capital and Class*, no. 8, 1979.

7 For a collection of papers which challenges this view see: S. Harding and M. Hintikka, eds, *Discovering Reality: Feminist Perspectives on Epistemology, Metaphysics, Methodology, and Philosophy of Science*, Reidel, Holland, 1983.

8 E. Spelman argues in favour of this point in relation to Aristotle's politics and ontology, in 'Aristotle and the Politicization of the Soul' in Harding and Hintikka, eds, *Discovering Reality*.

9 I am thinking here of the critiques of 'theory' made by earlier feminists who sometimes wrote as if theory *per se* were 'the enemy'. See, for example, the collection edited by B. and T. Roszack, *Masculine/Feminine: Readings in Sexual Mythology and the Liberation of Women*, Harper and Row, New York, 1969.

10 See S. Firestone, *The Dialectic of Sex*, Paladin, London, 1972, chapter 10; and S. de Beauvoir, *The Second Sex*, Penguin, Harmondsworth, 1975, pp. 735–41.

11 For example, see J. B. Elshtain, *Public Man, Private Woman*, Princeton University Press, Princeton, New Jersey, 1981; J. Grimshaw, *Philosophy and Feminist Thinking*, University of Minnesota Press, Minneapolis, 1986; T. de Lauretis *Feminist Studies/Critical Studies*, Indiana University Press, Bloomington, 1986; S. Benhabib and D. Cornell, eds, *Feminism as Critique*, University of Minnesota Press, Minneapolis, 1987; C. Pateman, *The Sexual Contract*, Polity Press, Cambridge, 1988; L. Nicholson, *Feminism/Postmodernism*, Routledge, London and New York, 1990. Each of these texts distinguishes itself by taking up an interrogative attitude to the traditional assumptions and paradigms of philosophy.

12 An excellent example of this form of theorizing is J. R. Martin's *Reclaiming a Conversation: The Ideal of the Educated Woman*, Yale University Press, New Haven and London, 1985.

13 C. McMillan, *Women, Reason and Nature: Some Philosophical Problems with Feminism*, Blackwell, Oxford, 1982.

14 E. Spelman in 'Woman as Body: Ancient and Contemporary Views' in *Feminist Studies*, 8, no. 1, 1982, offers an interesting account of the feminist desire for disembodiment.

15 No doubt men too suffer from this system. No matter how competent a (male) politician is taken to be, his career can be ruined by his sexual proclivities coming under public scrutiny. Presumably, 'the public' expects men to have sexual relations. However, they expect these to remain *private*.

16 G. W. F. Hegel, *The Phenomenology of Mind*, trans. J. B. Baillie, Harper and Row, New York, 1967, p. 496.

CHAPTER 1   But for her Sex, a Woman is a Man

1 Jean-Jacques Rousseau, *Emile*, Dent and Sons, London, 1972, p. 356.
2 Ibid., p. 349.
3 Ibid.

4 For example, Descartes and his followers assume that sexual difference is irrelevant to the soul and its capacity for reason. Although
   Descartes is careful to insist that the soul does not sit in the body like a
   pilot in his ship, he does not mean by this that the sex of the body
   would influence the form or nature of the soul.

5 *Emile*, p. 321.

6 Ibid., p. 324.

7 For example, see J. Abray, 'Feminism in the French Revolution',
   American Historical Review, 80, 1975; and especially, J. B. Landes,
   Women and the Public Sphere in the Age of the French Revolution,
   Cornell University Press, Ithaca, New York, 1988.

8 See chapter 5.

9. Mary Wollstonecraft, *A Vindication of the Rights of Woman* (1792),
   Penguin, Harmondsworth, 1975, p. 139.

10 Ibid., p. 142.

11 Ibid., p. 79.

12 Emile, p. 325.

13 J.-J. Rousseau, *Discourse on the Origin of Inequality*, in *The First and
    Second Discourses*, R. D. and J. R. Masters, eds, St Martin's Press,
    New York, 1964.

14 *Emile*, p. 339.

15 S. Moller Okin, *Women in Western Political Thought*, Virago,
    London, 1980, p. 99f.

16 Rousseau remarked: 'I had come to see that everything was radically
    connected with politics,' quoted in M. Cranston's introduction to *The
    Social Contract*, Penguin, Harmondsworth, 1975, p. 13.

17 *Emile*, p. 281.

18 Ibid., p. 172.

19 For an illuminating account of the body politic as analogous to a
    birth, see C. Pateman, 'The Fraternal Social Contract: Some Obser-
    vations on Patriarchal Civil Society' in J. Keane, ed., *Civil Society
    and the State: New European Perspectives*, Verso, London and New
    York, 1988.

20 *Social Contract*, p. 84.

21 *Emile*, p. 370.

22 Ibid., p. 442.

23 Ibid., p. 412.

24 Ibid., p. 321.

25 Ibid., p. 9.

26 Ibid., p. 57.

27 Ibid., see p. 328.

28 Ibid., see p. 173.

29 Ibid., p. 56.

30 Ibid., p. 299.

31 Ibid., p. 222.
32 Ibid., p. 53.
33 Ibid., p. 182.
34 *The Social Contract*, p. 66.
35 *Emile*, pp. 62–3.
36 Ibid., p. 63.
37 Ibid., p. 64 n. 1.
38 Ibid., p. 20.
39 Ibid., p. 364.
40 Ibid., p. 208.
41 See the tutor's observation concerning Sophy's mother who '. . . smiles at the success of our schemes', *Emile*, p. 378.
42 Ibid., p. 412.
43 *Social Contract*, p. 49.
44 See ibid., p. 187n.
45 *Emile*, p. 328.
46 Okin, *Women in Western Political Thought*, p. 130f.
47 *Emile*, p. 338.
48 Ibid., p. 345.
49 Ibid., p. 345.
50 Ibid., p. 340.
51 See ibid., p. 325 and p. 328.
52 Ibid., p. 328.
53 Ibid., p. 443.
54 Ibid., p. 326. Emphasis added.
55 Ibid., p. 324.
56 *Social Contract*, p. 134.
57 *Emile*, pp. 10–11.
58 *Social Contract*, p. 50.
59 Ibid., pp. 142–3.
60 *Emile*, p. 332.
61 Wollstonecraft, *Vindication*, p. 139. Emphasis added.
62 Ibid., pp. 142–3.
63 Ibid., p. 91.
64 Wollstonecraft locates man's superiority to 'brutes' in the rational capacity. See *Vindication*, p. 91.
65 Ibid., p. 142.
66 Ibid., p. 316.
67 Ibid., p. 103.
68 See ibid., p. 189.
69 See, for example, C. Pateman, *The Sexual Contract*, Polity Press, Cambridge, 1988, chapter 5.
70 Wollstonecraft, *Vindication*, p. 299.

CHAPTER 2   What the Human Species may be Made

1 *Utilitarianism*, Collins, London and Glasgow, 1970, p. 265.
2 *Nature, the Utility of Religion and Theism*, Watts and Co, London, 1904, pp. 24–5.
3 For a selection of the more vituperative of these views concerning Taylor's contributions to Mill's work, see A. Rossi, *Essays on Sex Equality*, University of Chicago Press, Chicago, 1970, pp. 31–45.
4 See my observations in chapter 3 concerning the relationship of de Beauvoir's work to Sartre's and, chapter 5.
5 S. Smith, quoted favourably by Taylor in 'Enfranchisement of Women' in Rossi, *Essays on Sex Equality*, p. 101n.
6 Ibid., p. 110. Emphasis added.
7 *The Subjection of Women*, in Rossi, *Essays on Sex Equality*, p. 234. Emphasis added.
8 See E. Shorter, *The Making of the Modern Family*, Collins, London, 1976.
9 *Subjection of Women*, pp. 148–9.
10 *Nature, the Utility of Religion and Theism*, p. 28. Emphasis added.
11 Ibid., p. 32.
12 Ibid., p. 33. Emphasis added.
13 See 'Essays on Marriage and Divorce' in Rossi, *Essays on Sex Equality*, p. 73.
14 This theme will be treated in more detail in chapter 3 and, especially, chapter 6.
15 See G. Kennedy, *The Psychological Empiricism of John Stuart Mill*, Amherst, Massachusetts, 1928, for an account of Mill's empirical psychologism.
16 'Enfranchisement of Women', p. 104. Emphasis added.
17 From *Principles of Political Economy*, quoted in Rossi, *Essays on Sex Equality*, p. 55. Emphasis added.
18 J. Locke, *Two Treatises of Government*, ed. P. Laslett, Mentor, New York, 1965, pp. 328–9. Emphasis in original.
19 C. B. Macpherson, *The Political Theory of Possessive Individualism*, O. U. P., London, 1975, p. 3. Emphasis added. See also pp. 263–4 where he summarizes these assumptions under seven points.
20 Although merely removing legal sanctions, as Mill suggests, would not be sufficient for women's emancipation if the economy remained structured as it is.
21 See his arguments on hardship in *Subjection of Women*, pp. 178–9.
22 See C. McMillan, *Women, Reason and Nature*, Blackwell, Oxford, 1982, chapter 1, for an interesting defence of women's work as

involving rationality and intentionality; and my discussion of her work in chapter 4.

23 *Utilitarianism*, p. 320.
24 'Essays on Marriage and Divorce', p. 74. Emphasis in original. That this is also Mill's mature view is clear from *Subjection of Women*, p. 178.
25 Ibid., p. 75.
26 *Subjection of Women*, p. 178.
27 'Essays on Marriage and Divorce', p. 76. Emphasis in original.
28 Ibid., p. 75. Emphasis in original.
29 Ibid., p. 76. Emphasis added.
30 See *Subjection of Women*, pp. 179f. It is significant that these 'exceptional circumstances' are dependent on the women possessing both genius and wealth.
31 Ibid., p. 179. Emphasis added.
32 *Subjection of Women*, p. 228. Emphasis added.
33 *On Liberty*, Penguin, Harmondsworth, 1976, p. 70. Emphasis added.
34 For an account of Mill's attitude to socialism see G. E. Panichas, 'Mill's Flirtation with Socialism and Communism' in *The Southern Journal of Philosophy*, vol. XXI, no. 2.
35 The importance that Mill attached to systematicity and consistency in his thought is well known and reflected in his own introspective observation that 'I never in the course of my transition was content to remain, for ever so short a time, confused and unsettled. When I had taken in any new idea, *I could not rest till I had adjusted its relation to my old opinions*, and ascertained exactly how far its effect ought to extend in modifying or superseding them.' J. J. Coss, ed., *Autobiography of John Stuart Mill*, Columbia University Press, New York, 1924, p. 110. Emphasis added.
36 For a detailed critique of Mill's account of the complementarity of the sexes see J. Annas, 'Mill and the Subjection of Women', in *Philosophy*, 52, 1977, pp. 179–94.
37 See Coss, *Autobiography of John Stuart Mill*.
38 See *Subjection of Women*, pp. 235–6.
39 See Coss, *Autobiography*, pp. 174–6 and F. Hayek, *John Stuart Mill and Harriet Taylor: Their Friendship and Subsequent Marriage*, University of Chicago Press, Chicago, 1951.
40 'Essays on Marriage and Divorce', See pp. 86, 103.
41 Ibid., p. 103. Emphasis added.
42 Ibid., p. 86. Emphasis added.
43 Ibid., p. 92. Emphasis added.
44 Mill, in correspondence with Taylor, writes: 'We must finish the best we have got to say, and not only that, but publish it while we are alive. I do not see what living depository there is likely to be of our

thoughts, or who in this *weak generation* that is growing up *will even be capable of thoroughly mastering and assimilating your ideas*, much less of re-originating them – so we must write them and print them, and then they can wait *until there are again thinkers*.' Hayek, *John Stuart Mill and Harriet Taylor*, p. 185. Emphasis added.

45 See, for example, 'Enfranchisement of Women', p. 105.

46 Ibid.

47 Though Mill comes very close to doing so in the example he uses concerning the labour of slaves, sailors and women. See *Subjection of Women*, p. 155.

48 See Rossi, *Essays on Sex Equality*, p. 37.

49 'Enfranchisement of Women', p. 104.

50 Macpherson, in *Political Theory of Possessive Individualism*, has a good account of how rationality becomes tied to property and wealth but he does not mention the role of women or domestic production at all!

51 *On Liberty*, pp. 68–9. Emphasis added.

52 For a detailed account of why this is so see L. M. G. Clark, 'Women and John Locke; or, Who Owns the Apples in the Garden of Eden?', *Canadian Journal of Philosophy*, vol. VII, no. 4, Dec. 1977, and C. Pateman and T. Brennan, ' "Mere Auxiliaries to the Commonwealth": Women and the Origins of Liberalism' in *Political Studies*, vol. 27, no. 2, 1979.

53 See *On Liberty*, pp. 81f, for his account of the method by which we may, progressively, approximate truth.

54 Ibid., p. 128.

55 Ibid., p. 69. See also *Subjection of Women*, p. 132.

56 See 'Essays on Marriage and Divorce', pp. 73–4.

57 Ibid., p. 73.

58 Ibid.

59 See *On Liberty*, p. 128.

60 See *Leviathan*, Penguin, Harmondsworth, 1986, pp. 253–4.

61 See *Two Treatises of Government*, Mentor, New York, 1965, pp. 364–5.

62 See *Discourse on the Origin of Inequality* in *The First and Second Discourses*, R. D. and J. R. Masters, eds, St Martin's Press, New York, 1964, where Rousseau describes women, in a state of nature, as men's equal.

63 'Essays on Marriage and Divorce', p. 73. Emphasis added.

CHAPTER 3   Woman as the Other

1 Simone de Beauvoir, *The Second Sex*, trans. H. M. Parshley, Penguin, Harmondsworth, 1975, p. 28.

2 J.-P. Sartre, *Being and Nothingness*, Methuen, London, 1977.
3 Ibid, p. 25; see also J.-P. Sartre, *Existentialism and Humanism*, Methuen, London, 1948.
4 *Being and Nothingness*, pp. 303f.
5 *The Second Sex*, p. 13.
6 I have discussed this issue in 'Feminism, Philosophy and Riddles Without Answers' in *Feminist Challenges: Social and Political Theory*, C. Pateman and E. Gross, eds, Allen and Unwin, Sydney, 1986. See also C. Mackenzie, 'Simone de Beauvoir: Philosophy and/or the Female Body' in *Feminist Challenges*, which acted as a stimulus for many of the ideas in this chapter.
7 *Second Sex*, pp. 28–9.
8 *Being and Nothingness*, pp. 47f.
9 See M. Le Doeuff, 'Operative Philosophy: Simone de Beauvoir and Existentialism' in *Ideology and Consciousness*, no. 6, Autumn, 1979. See, by same author, *The Philosophical Imaginary*, Athlone, London, 1989.
10 On the Hegelian and Sartrean influences on de Beauvoir's work see G. Lloyd, 'Masters, Slaves and Others' in *Radical Philosophy*, no. 34, 1983.
11 *The Second Sex*, p. 17.
12 Ibid., p. 21.
13 Ibid., p. 93.
14 Ibid., p. 31.
15 Ibid., p. 287.
16 Ibid., p. 96.
17 Ibid., p. 61.
18 Ibid., p. 285.
19 Ibid., p. 286.
20 Ibid., p. 355.
21 Ibid., p. 356.
22 Ibid., pp. 94–5.
23 Ibid., pp. 95–6.
24 Ibid., p. 94.
25 Ibid., p. 208.
26 Ibid., p. 359. Emphasis added.
27 Ibid., pp. 406–7.
28 See M. Collins and C. Pierce, 'Holes and Slime: Sexism in Sartre's Psychoanalysis' in C. Gould and M. Wartofsky, eds, *Women and Philosophy*, Capricorn Books, New York, 1976.
29 *Being and Nothingness*, p. 609.
30 Ibid., p. 613.
31 *Second Sex*, p. 723.
32 Ibid., p. 21.

33 In the original: 'La dévaluation de la femme représente une étape nécessaire dans l'histoire de l'humanité', *Le Deuxième Sexe*, Gallimard, Paris, 1949, vol. I, p. 125.
34 In the original: '. . . la dévaluation de la féminité a été une étape nécessaire de l'evolution humaine . . .', ibid., vol. II, p. 563.
35 *The Second Sex*, p. 727.
36 Ibid., p. 741.
37 *Being and Nothingness*, p. 578.
38 *Second Sex*, p. 728. Emphasis added.
39 See *Portrait of the Anti-Semite*, Secker and Warburg, New York, 1948.

CHAPTER 4   Language, Facts and Values

1 See Alison Jaggar, *Feminist Politics and Human Nature*, Harvester Press, Brighton, 1983, part 2.
2 Janet Radcliffe Richards, *The Sceptical Feminist*, Penguin, Harmondsworth, 1982, see her source quoted in chapter 10, n. 7.
3 See Elshtain, *Public Man, Private Woman*; and C. Pateman, 'Feminist Critiques of the Public/Private Dichotomy', in S. Benn and G. Gaus, eds, *Public and Private in Social Life*, Croom Helm, London, 1983.
4 Richards, *Sceptical Feminist*, p. 13.
5 Ibid.
6 Ibid., p. 17.
7 See G. Lloyd, *The Man of Reason: 'Male' and 'Female' in Western Philosophy*, Methuen, London, 1984.
8 Richards, *Sceptical Feminist*, p. 18.
9 Analytic philosophy's conception of itself as a discourse of legitimation or foundation, whether of claims to knowledge or concepts of justice, has been widely criticised in recent times, notably by Richard Rorty in *Philosophy and the Mirror of Nature*, Blackwell, Oxford, 1980. Among philosophers from outside the analytic tradition Nietzsche stands out as the one who makes questions of value central to philosophy: the task of philosophy, on his view, involves calling into question the value of moral values, and even of truth itself. See *On the Genealogy of Morals*, Vintage Books, New York, 1969, Preface, 6; III, 27.
10 Richards, *Sceptical Feminist*, p. 195.
11 Ibid., p. 198.
12 Ibid., p. 199.
13 Ibid.
14 Ibid. Emphasis added.

15 Ibid., p. 206.
16 Ibid., p. 221.
17 John Rawls, *A Theory of Justice*, Clarendon Press, Oxford, 1972.
18 S. Moller Okin, 'Justice and Gender', in *Philosophy and Public Affairs*, vol. 16, no. 1, 1987.
19 Rawls, *Theory of Justice*, p. 129.
20 Moller Okin, 'Justice and Gender', p. 50.
21 Richards, *Sceptical Feminist*, p. 19.
22 Carol McMillan, *Women, Reason and Nature*, Blackwell, Oxford, 1982, p. x.
23 Ibid., see pp. 52–3, 56.
24 Ibid., p. 63.
25 Ibid., p. 81.
26 Ibid., p. 60.
27 Ibid., p. 84. Emphasis added.
28 Ibid., see chapter 5.
29 Ibid., p. 64.
30 See chapter 6, below.
31 McMillan, *Women, Reason and Nature*, p. 95.
32 See A. Rich, *Of Woman Born*, Norton and Co., New York, 1976.
33 McMillan, *Women, Reason and Nature*, p. 108.
34 See E. Shorter, *The Making of the Modern Family*, Collins, London, 1976.
35 McMillan, *Women, Reason and Nature*, p. 87. Emphasis added.
36 Rich, *Of Woman Born*, p. xvi.
37 Ibid., p. 15
38 Ibid., p. 286.
39 McMillan, *Women, Reason and Nature*, see p. 54, 56.
40 See, for example, her comments on chemical contraception and medical practices in labour wards, ibid., pp. 132–46.
41 See Rich, *Of Woman Born* and M. Daly, *Gyn/Ecology: The Metaethics of Radical Feminism*, Beacon Press, Boston, 1978.
42 McMillan, *Women, Reason and Nature*; see, for example, p. 79n.
43 Ibid., p. 147.
44 Ibid., p. 104.
45 Ibid., p. 103.
46 Dale Spender, *Man Made Language* (1980), Routledge and Kegan Paul, London, second edition, 1985, p. x.
47 Benjamin Whorf, *Language, Thought and Reality: Selected Writings*, J. B. Carrol, ed., MIT Press, Cambridge, Mass., 1976.
48 Spender, *Man Made Language*, p. 139. Emphasis in original.
49 Ibid., p. 164.
50 Richards, *Sceptical Feminist*, p. 143. Emphasis in original.
51 Ibid., see p. 132.

52 Spender, *Man Made Language*, p. 142.
53 Ibid., p. 77. Emphasis added.
54 See, for example, Spender's comments pp. 147–50.
55 On this see A. Assiter, 'Did Man Make Language?' in *Radical Philosophy*, no. 34, 1983.
56 Spender, *Man Made Language*, p. 31.
57 Ibid., pp. 4–5.
58 Ibid., p. 189. Emphasis added.
59 Daly, *Gyn/Ecology*, p. 112.
60 Ibid., p. 55.
61 Ibid., p. 112.
62 For example, ibid., pp. 323–33.
63 Ibid., p. 30.
64 Ibid., p. 62
65 Ibid, p. 17.
66 Grimshaw, *Philosophy and Feminist Thinking*, p. 126.
67 Although I agree with Grimshaw's claims concerning Daly's fascistic tendencies, I do not agree that Daly derives these from Nietzsche's philosophy. Nor do I agree with Grimshaw's description of Nietzsche's project as the *inversion* of Christian values. See above, n. 9.
68 Elshtain, *Public Man, Private Woman*, p. 209.
69 Daly, *Gyn/Ecology*, p. 298. Emphasis added.
70 Ibid., p. 312.
71 Ibid., p. 8.
72 Ibid, p. 355.
73 Ibid, p. 14.
74 Ibid, p. 350.
75 See M. Morris, 'A-mazing Grace: Notes on Mary Daly's Poetics' in *Intervention*, no. 16, 1982; reprinted in *The Pirate's Fiancée*, Verso, London and New York, 1988, for a sophisticated and sympathetic reading of *Gyn/Ecology*. Morris offers a convincing argument concerning the repetition of mythic structures in Daly's account of patriarchal culture.
76 Daly, *Gyn/Ecology*, pp. 12–13.
77 Daly generally uses the upper case *Self* for the 'true' self and the lower case *self* for the 'false' self.
78 Daly, *Gyn/Ecology*, p. 14.
79 Ibid., see pp. 344–5.
80 De Lauretis, *Feminist Studies/Critical Studies*, p. 13.

CHAPTER 5   The Feminist Critique of Philosophy

1 The phrase 'quantum leap' is used in a similar sense by A. Rich, in *On Lies, Secrets and Silence*, Virago, London, 1980, pp. 271f.

2 V. Solanas, 'The S.C.U.M. Manifesto' in *Masculine/Feminine*, B. Roszack and T. Roszack, eds, Harper and Row, New York, 1969, p. 265.

3 M. Daly, *Gyn/Ecology: The Metaethics of Radical Feminism*, Beacon Press, Boston, 1978. See introduction and p. 112, for example.

4 See chapter 6 below.

5 Michéle le Doeuff, 'Women and Philosophy' in *Radical Philosophy*, no. 17 Summer, 1977, p. 2.

6 Daly, *Gyn/Ecology*, p. 381.

7 D. Spender, *Man Made Language* (1980), Routledge and Kegan Paul, London, second edition, 1985, p. 142.

8 Ibid., p. 4. Emphasis added.

9 Ibid., see pp. 102–5.

10 See chapter 3, Woman as the Other.

11 K. Marx, 'The German Ideology' in *The Marx-Engels Reader*, R. C. Tucker, ed, Norton and Co., New York, 1972, pp. 136–7.

12 For example, le Doeuff, 'Women and Philosophy', and G. Lloyd, *The Man of Reason*, particularly chapter 7.

13 M. Wollstonecraft, *A Vindication of the Rights of Woman*, Penguin, Harmondsworth, 1975, p. 103. Emphasis added.

14 Ibid., see p. 189.

15 N. Jay, 'Gender and Dichotomy', *Feminist Studies*, 7, no. 1, Spring, 1981.

16 Ibid., p. 47.

17 N. Chodorow, *The Reproduction of Mothering: Psychoanalysis and the Sociology of Gender*, University of California Press, Berkeley, 1978.

18 Lloyd, *The Man of Reason*, especially chapters 1 and 2.

19 Ibid., p. ix.

20 Ibid., see pp. 103f.

21 J.-J. Rousseau, *Emile*, Dent and Sons, London, 1972, p. 354.

22 J.-J. Rousseau, '*Discourse on the Origin of Inequality*', in R. D. and J. R. Masters, eds, *The First and Second Discourses*, St Martin's Press, New York, 1964.

23 J.-J. Rousseau, *Politics and the Arts: A Letter to D'Alembert on the Theatre*, Cornell University Press, New York, 1968, p. 109.

24 D. Hume, *A Treatise of Human Nature*, L. A. Selby-Bigge, ed., Clarendon Press, Oxford, 1968, book III, part II.

25 G. W. F. Hegel, *The Phenomenology of Mind*, trans. J. B. Baillie, Harper and Row, New York, 1967, p. 496.

26 R. Descartes, 'The Principles of Philosophy' in *The Philosophical Works of Descartes*, trans. E. S. Haldane and G. R. T. Ross, Cambridge University Press, 1970, vol. 1, pp. 211–13.

27 For an explanation of this conception see J. Henriques, W. Hollway, C. Urwin, C. Venn and V. Walkerdine, *Changing the Subject*, Methuen, London, 1984.

28 For example, A. Rich, *Of Woman Born*, Norton and Co., New York, 1976; L. Irigaray, *This Sex Which is Not One*, Cornell University Press, New York, 1985.

CHAPTER 6   Psychoanalysis and French Feminisms

1 See *Civilization and its Discontents* in *The Standard Edition of the Complete Psychological Works of Sigmund Freud*, trans. J. Strachey and others, Hogarth Press, London, 1978 (hereafter S. E.), vol. XXI; *Totem and Taboo*, in S. E. vol. XIII; *The Future of an Illusion*, S. E. vol. XXI; and *Moses and Monotheism*, S. E. vol. XXIII.

2 Freud's work on hysteria – which he once described as 'the mysterious leap from the mind to the body' – is a good example of his attempts to escape a hard mind/body dualism. See *Studies on Hysteria*, in S. E., vol. II; and *A Case of Hysteria* (Dora), in S. E. vol. VII. Likewise, his various topographies of mental life maintain that rationality and consciousness comprise a very small part of what is ordinarily called the 'mind'. See *Papers on Metapsychology*, S. E. vol. XIV and *The Ego and the Id*, S. E. vol. XIX.

3 Freud claims that 'a unity comparable to the ego cannot exist in the individual from the start; the ego has to be developed' in *On Narcissism*, S. E. vol. XIV, p. 77.

4 See J. Laplanche and J.-B. Pontalis, *The Language of Psychoanalysis*, Norton and Co., New York, 1973, pp. 214–16.

5 Freud, *The Unconscious*, S. E. vol. XIV, p. 177.

6 Freud, *Three Essays on the Theory of Sexuality*, S. E. vol. VII, p. 168.

7 J. Mitchell, *Psychoanalysis and Feminism*, Penguin, Harmondsworth, 1975.

8 Ibid., p. 413.

9 Ibid., p. xv.

10 Whereas socialization theory assumes a pre-existent subject who is subjected to various kinds of conditioning and training, psychoanalysis maintains that appropriate masculine and feminine behaviours are intrinsic to the construction of men and women as particular kinds of subjects.

11 Mitchell, *Psychoanalysis and Feminism*, p. xvi.

12 Ibid., p. 402.

13 Freud, *Civilization and its Discontents*, S. E. vol. XXI.

14 See Freud, *Some Psychical Consequences of the Anatomical Distinction Between the Sexes*, S. E. vol. XIX; *Three Essays*, S. E. vol. VII; and *Fetishism*, S. E. vol. XXI.

15 I have discussed this issue in 'Woman and her Double(s): Sex, Gender and Ethics', in *Australian Feminist Studies*, no. 10, Summer, 1989.

16 Freud, *Anatomical Distinction Between the Sexes*, p. 257.

17 See Freud, *Female Sexuality*, S. E. vol. XXI, p. 226 and *Femininity*, S. E. vol. XXII.

18 Freud, *Female Sexuality*, p. 236.

19 Freud, *Anatomical Distinction Between the Sexes*, p. 253.

20 Freud, *Femininity*, pp. 133–5.

21 Freud, *Anatomical Distinction Between the Sexes*, p. 256

22 Freud, *Femininity*, p. 135.

23 Freud, *Infantile Genital Organization*, S. E. XIX p. 145. Emphasis added.

24 Following Jane Gallop, I am inclined to be disrespectful of the penis/phallus distinction. See her essay 'Phallus/Penis: Same Difference' in *Thinking Through the Body*, Columbia University Press, New York, 1988.

25 See, for example, L. Irigaray, 'The Blind Spot of an Old Dream of Symmetry' in *Speculum of the Other Woman*, trans. G. C. Gill, Cornell University Press, Ithaca, New York, 1985, and 'When Our Lips Speak Together' in *This Sex Which is Not One*, trans. C. Porter and C. Burke, Cornell University Press, Ithaca, New York, 1985.

26 Freud, *Dissolution of the Oedipus Complex*, S. E. Vol. XIX, p. 178.

27 See Freud, *The Unconscious*.

28 Mitchell, *Psychoanalysis and Feminism*, p. 403.

29 See L. Althusser, 'Ideology and Ideological State Apparatuses' in *Lenin and Philosophy*, New Left Books, London, 1977.

30 For an interesting and sympathetic account of the problems with Althusser's account of ideology see P. Ricoeur, *Lectures on Ideology and Utopia*, G. H. Taylor, ed., Columbia University Press, New York, 1986, chapters 7, 8 and 9.

31 Mitchell, *Psychoanalysis and Feminism*, p. 409.

32 'The Fraternal Social Contract' in J. Keane, ed., *Civil Society and the State: New European Perspectives*, Verso, London, 1988. See also C. Pateman, *The Sexual Contract*, Polity Press, Cambridge, 1988, especially chapter 2.

33 See J. Gallop, *Feminism and Psychoanalysis: the Daughter's Seduction*, MacMillan Press, London, 1982, chapter 1, for a detailed criticism of Mitchell's oversight.

34 *Psychoanalysis and Feminism*, pp. 382–98.

35 See E. D. Gelfand and V. T. Hules, *French Feminist Criticism*, Garland Publishing Inc., New York, London, 1985; M. Poovey, 'Feminism and Deconstruction' in *Feminist Studies*, 14, no. 1, Spring, 1988; R. Tong, *Feminist Thought*, Westview Press, Boulder, Colorado, 1989, chapter 8; and E. Grosz, *Sexual Subversions*, Allen and Unwin, Sydney, 1989.

36 M. Foucault, *Power/Knowledge*, C. Gordon, ed., Harvester Press, Brighton, 1980, p. 118.

37 T. Moi, *Sexual/Textual Politics: Feminist Literary Theory*, Methuen, London, 1985, p. 96

38 See J. Lacan, *Ecrits: A Selection*, Tavistock, London, 1977. For an accessible appraisal of Lacan's influence on French feminisms see Grosz, *Sexual Subversions*.

39 'Women and Literature in France', in *Signs*, vol. 3, no. 4, 1978.

40 See J. Derrida, *Spurs: Nietzsche's Styles*, University of Chicago Press, Chicago, 1981. A commentary which may be useful is J. Culler, *On Deconstruction: Theory and Criticism After Structuralism*, Cornell University Press, Ithaca, New York, 1982.

41 V. Hules, 'A Topography of Difference' in Gelfand and Hules, *French Feminist Criticism*, p. xix.

42 On writing the body, see M. Gagnon, 'Body I' in *New French Feminisms*, E. Marks and I. Courtivron, eds, University of Massachusetts Press, Amherst, 1980. Also M. Wittig, *The Guérillères*, Picador, London, 1971; M. Duras, *The Ravishing of Lol V. Stein*, Grove Press, New York, 1966.

43 On this, see: Freud, *The Unconscious*, pp. 201–2; *The Interpretation of Dreams*, S. E. vol. V, p. 601; *Repression*, S. E. vol. XIV, p. 152.

44 Moi, *Sexual/Textual Politics*, p. 98. Emphasis added.

45 Ibid. p. 97.

46 See my paper, 'A Critique of the Sex/Gender Distinction' in *Beyond Marxism? Interventions After Marx*, J. Allen and P. Patton, eds, Intervention Publications, Sydney, 1983, reprinted in *A Feminist Reader*, S. Gunew, ed., Routledge, London, 1990; Sandra Harding, 'Why has the Sex/Gender System Become Visible Only Now?' in *Discovering Reality*, Harding and Hintikka, eds.

47 See Irigaray, 'This Sex Which is Not One' in *This Sex Which is Not One*.

48 Irigaray, 'The Power of Discourse and the Subordination of the Feminine' in *This Sex Which is Not One*, p. 78.

49 Irigaray, 'Women's Exile' in *Ideology and Consciousness*, no. 1, 1977, p. 62.

50 During times when the church was the 'public' arena, women were bid to 'be silent in church'. The silencing of women during the French

revolution was accomplished, often enough, by literal decapitation.

51   Irigaray, 'Women On the Market' in *This Sex Which is Not One*.

52   I am indebted to one of Polity's anonymous readers for suggesting this connection between Lacan's formulation of the Symbolic and social contract theory. On Lacan's account it is language that forms the basis of the social contract. The differentiation between the sexes in the Symbolic excludes women from social agency in a manner that duplicates the structure of the social contract. On this issue see D. Macey, *Lacan in Contexts*, Verso, London and New York, 1988. Macey presents an interesting case for the relentless phallocentrism of Lacan and argues against the utility of Lacanian psychoanalysis to feminism. Obviously, many feminists do not share his viewpoint.

53   'Constructing the Subject: Deconstructing the Text' in *Feminist Criticism and Social Change*, J. Newton and D. Rosenfelt, eds, Methuen, London, 1985, p. 50.

54   See Lacan, 'The Mirror Stage as Formative of the Function of the I' in *Ecrits*.

55   Ibid.

56   Irigaray, 'The Power of Discourse' in *This Sex Which is Not One*, p. 73. See also 'Questions' in ibid., p. 123 and 'Women's Exile' in *Ideology and Consciousness*, p. 69.

57   Cixous, 'Castration or Decapitation?' in *Signs*, vol. 7, no. 1, 1981.

58   De Beauvoir, *The Second Sex*, Penguin, Harmondsworth, 1975, p. 21

59   Irigaray, 'Questions' in *This Sex Which is Not One*, pp. 129–30.

60   Irigaray, 'Women's Exile', p. 76.

61   See A. Dworkin, *Intercourse*, Free Press, New York, 1987, for a recent example of a feminist reduction of heterosexuality to the model of rape.

62   Cixous, 'Castration or Decapitation?', p. 52.

CHAPTER 7   Sexual Difference or Sexual Equality?

1   For example, Mary O'Brien, *The Politics of Reproduction*, Routledge and Kegan Paul, London, 1981; Nancy Hartsock, *Money, Sex and Power*, Longman, New York, 1983; and especially, Carole Pateman, *The Sexual Contract*, Polity Press, Cambridge, 1988.

2   T. Hobbes, *Leviathan*, pp. 81–2. Here, as below, I have rendered the English modern.

3   Ibid., p. 186.

4   Ibid., pp. 720–1.

5   Here I differ from Pateman's understanding of women's status in the body politic. She argues that 'women both are and are not part of the

civil order', *Sexual Contract*, p. 181. Her view is that in so far as the marriage contract is a civil contract, wives must be civil subjects. I am more inclined to question the validity rather than stress the paradoxical nature of the marriage contract.

6   David Hume, *An Enquiry Concerning the Principles of Morals*, L. A. Selby-Bigge, ed., Clarendon Press, Oxford, 1975, p. 191. Emphasis added.

7   See 'Land Rights: Aboriginal Land Rights and the Need for a National Policy', National Aborigines Conference, reprinted in *Dispossession: Black Australians and White Invaders*, compiled by Henry Reynolds, Allen and Unwin, Sydney, 1989, pp. 88–92.

8   For example, Hobbes argued that labour does not entitle ownership in the pre-political state, where might equals right. Locke, on the other hand, would argue that labour and possession go hand in hand in the pre-political state. In the present context I am not so interested in these differences. Rather, I am interested in the similarities in the attitudes of traditional political theorists towards women and their relation to labour, possession and property.

9   J. Locke, *Two Treatises of Government*, Mentor, New York, 1965, p. 328. Emphasis in original.

10   Rousseau, for example, stresses the inferiority of the freedom to follow impulse in the state of nature compared with the freedom to develop and follow reason in the body politic.

11   F. Engels, *The Origin of the Family, Private Property and the State*, Progress Publishers, Moscow, 1972, p. 73. Emphasis added.

12   Ibid., p. 71.

13   Hobbes, *Leviathan*, p. 151. Emphasis in original.

14   Ibid., p. 264.

15   *Emile*, pp. 62–3.

16   See, for example, Marx's *Economic and Philosophic Manuscripts of 1844* in R. Tucker, ed., *The Marx-Engels Reader*, Norton and Co., New York, 1972, pp. 62–3.

17   For example, see M. Barrett, *Women's Oppression Today*, pp. 172–86.

18   *Emile*, p. 324.

19   In his personal life – if not in his theory – Mill did categorically reject the inequity of the marriage contract. Mill's unofficial 'contract' with Taylor runs as follows: '. . . the whole character of the marriage relation as constituted by law being such as both she and I entirely and conscientiously disapprove, for this among other reasons, that it confers upon one of the parties to the contract, legal power and control over the person, property, and freedom of action of the other party, independent of her own wishes and will; I, having no means of legally divesting myself of these odious powers . . . feel it my duty to

put on record a formal protest against the existing law of marriage, in so far as conferring such powers; and a solemn promise never in any case or under any circumstances to use them.' Quoted in A. Rossi, *Essays in Sex Equality*, p. 45.

20   *The Second Sex*, p. 13.

21   Indeed, this has already taken place to some extent: the proliferation of laundromats, restaurants, escort agencies and child-minding centres in the last twenty or so years. Of course, these services are almost exclusively 'manned' by women.

22   M. Foucault, *The History of Sexuality*, vol. I, Allen Lane, London, 1979, p. 78.

23   *The Second Sex*, p. 696.

24   Ibid., p. 697.

25   *The Dialectic of Sex*, p. 223.

26   Rich, 'Compulsory Heterosexuality and Lesbian Existence' (1980), reprinted in *Blood, Bread and Poetry: Selected Prose 1979–1985*, Virago, London, 1986, p. 57. Note also the Afterword to this paper, pp. 68–75.

27   See Foucault, *The History of Sexuality*, p. 77.

28   D.-A.-F. de Sade, *Justine, Philosophy in the Bedroom and Other Writings*, Grove Press, New York, 1965, p. 249. Emphasis added.

29   Angela Carter in *The Sadian Woman*, Virago, London, 1979, makes several pertinent comments on this theme.

30   'Enfranchisement of Women' in A. Rossi, *Essays in Sex Equality*, p. 105. Emphasis added.

31   See A. Game and R. Pringle, *Gender at Work*, Allen and Unwin, Sydney, 1983.

32   Carter, *The Sadian Woman*, p. 58. Emphasis added.

CONCLUSION

1   A recent and very interesting paper on this subject is Iris Young, 'The Ideal of Community and the Politics of Difference' in *Feminism/ Postmodernism*, L. J. Nicholson, ed., Routledge, New York and London, 1990.

2   See my paper, 'Towards a Feminist Philosophy of the Body', in *Crossing Boundaries: Feminisms and the Critique of Knowledges*, B. Caine, E. A. Grosz and M. de Lepervanche, eds, Allen and Unwin, Sydney, 1988, where I explore the possibility of a feminist reading of B. Spinoza's monistic philosophy.

3   For example, see *Australian Feminist Studies*, no. 5, on Feminism and the Body, and no. 10, on Sex and Gender; J. Gallop, *Thinking Through the Body*, Columbia University Press, 1988; and S.

Suleiman, ed., *The Female Body in Western Culture*, Harvard University Press, 1986.

4 See Pateman, *The Sexual Contract*, p. 96, where she states that 'according to the classic contract theorists, [women] are naturally deficient in a specifically *political* capacity, the capacity to create and maintain political right.' Emphasis in original.

5 A. MacIntyre, *After Virtue: A Study in Moral Theory*, (1981), Duckworth, London, second edition, 1985, p. 268.

6 For an account of the contrast between traditional understandings of the term 'power' and the Foucauldian understanding – which I am here endorsing – see P. Patton, 'Taylor and Foucault on Power and Freedom', *Political Studies*, vol. XXXVII, no. 2, 1989, especially pp. 268–74.

Index